CW01429490

How to Avoid False Accusations of Rape

Self Defense in the Feminist State

John Davis BA JD LLM

How to Avoid False Accusations of Rape:

Self Defense in the Feminist State

John Davis, BA., J.D., LL.M.

Old Town Publishing

ISBN-13: 978-1-507799055

ISBN-10: 1507799055

Library of Congress Cataloging-in-Publication Data

How To Avoid False Accusations of Rape / authored by Davis, BA, JD, LLM, John.

p. cm.

ISBN: 978-1-310-85897-0

1. Rape Reporting. 2. Rape. 3. Rape-United States I. Davis BA, JD, LLM, John, 1953 - .

342. D38575 2015

00-013243

10 9 8 7 6 5 4 3 2 1 2 3 4 5 6 7 8 9 10

DEDICATION

This book is dedicated to the over 10,000 men who were unjustly lynched in the "Jim Crow Era" from 1867 to the modern day, based upon false accusations. This book is also dedicated to all who work with victims of prejudice and bigotry, those who tirelessly strive for equality based upon race, gender or creed, and those who have, through the struggles of the United States of America, left an indelible mark on the progress of freedom, liberty and egalitarianism.

Jus Gentium: omnes homines naturâ æquales sunt.

("The Law of the People: All human beings are created equal").

"Ei incumbit probatio qui dicit, non qui negat"

("The burden of proof is on the person accusing, not upon the person who denies the accusation.") [A man is innocent until proven guilty – from the Justinian Code (Digest of Justinian 22.3.2).]

"False accusations of rape are not about sex . . . . like the crime of rape itself, false accusations of rape are about power." John Davis, B.A., J.D., LL.M.

ACKNOWLEDGMENTS

The Author and Publisher would like to thank Janet Bloomfield, Dr. Tara J. Palmatier, Psy.D., Deepika Narayan Bhardwaj, "The intrepid" Cathy Young, and Jyoti Tiwari for their insights into the injustices caused by false accusations of rape.

Table of Contents

HOW TO AVOID FALSE ACCUSATIONS OF RAPE:
SELF-DEFENSE IN THE FEMINIST STATE

John Davis[1]

PROLOGUE:
Situation Awareness

Men, as a gender, are increasingly under assault in modern "civilization."

There are societal pressures to require wom-

[1] *Bacheloris Artis*, Case Western Reserve University 1975; *Juris Doctor*, Seattle University School of Law 1981; *Legis Magister*, New York University School of Law 1984.

en to receive as much pay as men, while, at the same time, men are working demonstrably longer hours than women, and, 98% of on-the job deaths are sustained by men.

Men are being put in prison and jails at an astonishing rate, while women escape arrest, prosecution and accountability for the same crimes. When women *are* committed to jail or prison, they have, on the average, punishment that is only one-third of the prison sentences that men receive for the same crime.

In the area of human sexuality, men are being demonized, by rape hysteria, as predetermined serial rapists. Driven by fear and ignorance, more and more financial and political pressure is being exerted on institutions to place responsibility on men for any and all problems associated with human sexuality between men and women. These concerted pressures have all of the earmarks of a pogrom against men, masculinity and male sexuality. Our culture now, in the mainstream media, seeks to criminalize men as a gender.

This demonization of men, perpetuating the myth that "all men are rapists" is occurring at an accelerated rate, and, at a time when the actual rates of reported rape have been cut in half over the last forty years.

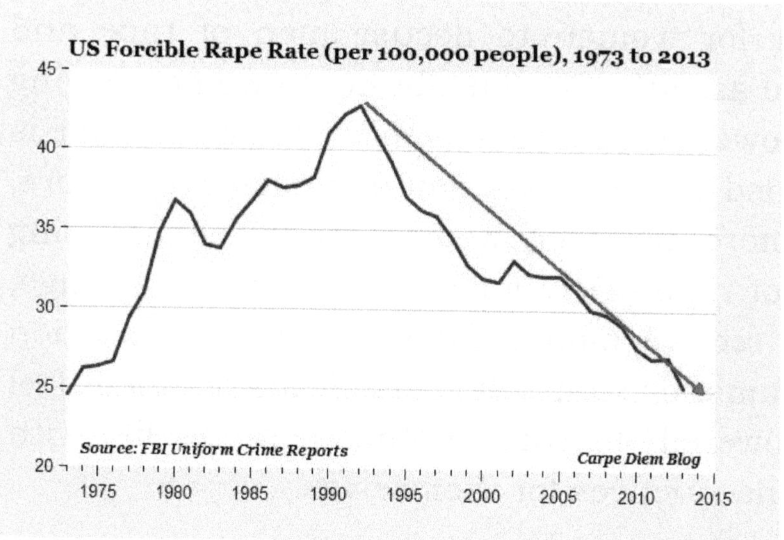

Figure 1 - Uniform FBI crime reports show a marked decline in reported forcible rape in the U.S. over the past 40 years.

In addition to all of these gender based assaults on men, gynocentric[2] political pressures are now lobbying for strict criminal liability for men, in any case in which a man and a woman share intimacy, and in which the woman is displeased. If this sounds as if it is an overstatement, the reader is invited to continue reading to the following chapters on "affirmative consent laws."

---

[2] *Gynocentric*, Syllabification: gy·no·cen·tric ADJECTIVE: Centered on or concerned exclusively with women; taking a female (or specifically a feminist) point of view. Oxford English Dictionary (2014).

As an integral part of this pogrom against men, our culture is promoting more and more power for women to accuse men of rape and sexual assault. No one objects to women having the power to accuse someone of crime – that is provided a crime has actually occurred. More, and more, however, women are falsely accusing men of rape solely for attention, or for revenge, or to receive money from victim compensation programs, or simply because it makes them feel "empowered" to ruin another person's life with no consequences for themselves.

Our research of government statistics indicates that the rate of false accusations of rape now exceed 60% of cases reported to law enforcement. This statistic is so hated by gynocentric groups, and misandrist groups, that the statistic is "shouted down" in the mainstream media at every opportunity. Nevertheless, Uniform FBI Crime Reports show, as a hard statistic, that law enforcement determines 8% of rape claims, each year, are false – law enforcement also determines that another 50% of rape claims are so meritless that they will not support the minimal requirements for an arrest. This 58% false rape claim statistic has been verified, over and over, by the only scientific studies ever applied to the subject.

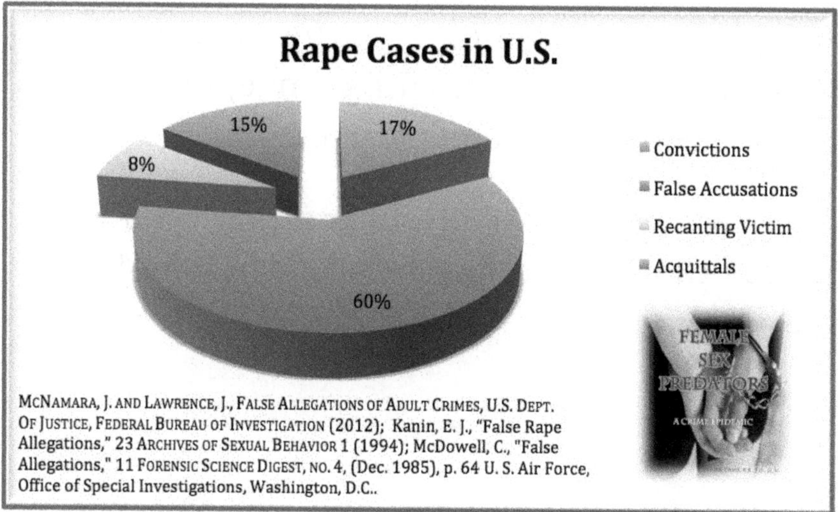

Figure 2 - This chart was prepared from a variety of statistics compiled from U. S. Department of Justice reports. The cited studies provide the scientific methods for analyzing the phenomenon of false rape reporting.

In reporting this rate of false accusations of rape, it is important to acknowledge that there is a plethora of pundits, advocacy research and mainstream media publicity that denies that the rate of making false accusations of rape is any higher than any other crime. Those mainstream media assertions, and advocacy research, that place the rate of false accusations of rape at between 2 and 8 percent, are simply based upon superstitions, misandry, gynosympathy and, in some cases, concerted efforts to deceive the public as to the actual rate of false accusations of rape.[3] These myths, superstitions, and outright false representations of the real rate of false accusations, are creating an epidemic of false rape accusations against men.

There are a number of cultural and political influences that are driving this epidemic of false accusations.

Hypoagency[4] – "I'm a woman – I'm not accountable."

First, and foremost, of the factors driving epidemic rates of false rape accusations, is the fact that women have little or no accountability for making false accusations of rape. Experienced prosecutors rarely, if ever, file charges against women who file false rape claims.

---

[3] Edward Greer, "*The Truth behind Legal Dominance Feminism's Two Percent False Rape Claim Figure*," 33 Loy. L.A. L. Rev. 947 (2000). Available at: http://digitalcommons.lmu.edu/llr/vol33/iss3/3

[4] *Hypoagency* is the feminist/patriarchal notion that women are not accountable or responsible for their wrongdoing because they are childlike and unable to make their own decisions or choices.

There are several reasons charges are rarely filed. In most states, the crime of making a false charge of rape is little more than a misdemeanor (usually false police reporting) that carries little more than a fine or community service on a conviction of a first offense. For many prosecutors, it is simply not worth the time, effort and professional commitment to pursue charges against women who make false accusations of rape.

Second, many (perhaps most) of those working in the legal system hold to the preposterous superstition that prosecuting women for filing false rape claims will somehow deter women with legitimate rape claims from filing rape complaints with law enforcement. This superstition, literally, has not one shred of evidence to support it. It is merely part of a cultural blindspot that promotes false accusations of rape, and, which denies men the equal protection of the laws.

Prosecutors have the discretion whether to charge someone with a crime they know has been committed. They are not required to prosecute every crime that appears on their desk. They are, however, required to avoid a pattern of discriminating against a group of victims based purely upon gender. We were unable to find even one single case of a man falsely accusing a woman of rape. Falsely accusing someone of rape is exclusively a crime committed by women, and, is almost exclusively a crime committed against men. Consequently, any pattern of refusal by prosecutors to prosecute women, for making false accusations of rape, invariably denies men (the sole victims of the crime) equal protection of the laws.[5]

The vast majority of people, according to our research, believe that false accusations of rape are a crime as serious as rape itself.

[5] Most importantly, it denies men the right to seek restitution from the criminal court system in the U.S. for the often devastating injuries incurred from false accusations of rape.

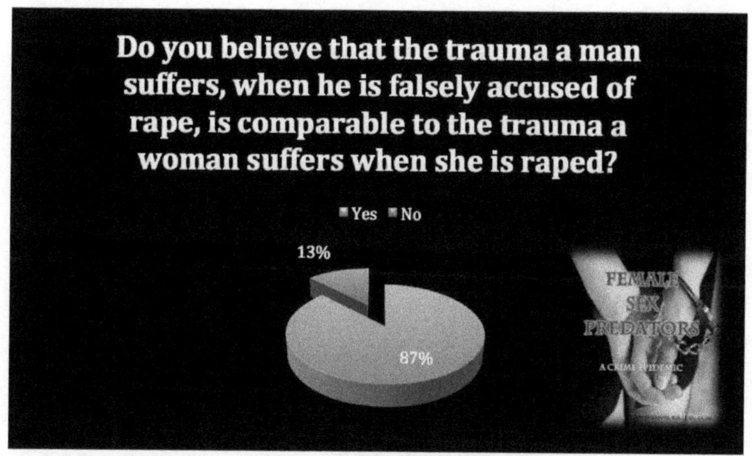

Data: Total responses: 160 Duration: 48 hours

Gender Distribution:
Male: 76% Avg. Completion time: 22 sec
Female: 24%

Indeed, criminologists and lawyers believe that a false accusation of rape causes just as much, or more, injury as rape itself. People surveyed in our informal polls indicated that they thought that any discussion of "rape culture" must include the phenomenon of false accusation epidemics that are plaguing our modern consciousness.

Poll Results Sunday 11 August 2014

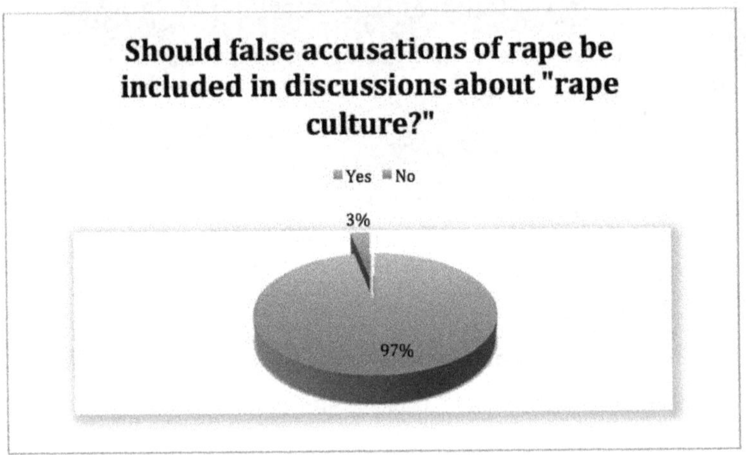

Data: Total responses:	211	Duration: 48 hours
Gender Distribution:		
Male:	78%	Avg. Completion time: 00:49 seconds
Female:	22%	

In many ways, false accusations of rape are a mirror crime of the crime of rape itself. False accusations of rape, like rape itself, are crimes that are motivated by rage and a desire to exert harm and power over the victim. It may be appropriate to label false accusations of rape as a sex crime - a form of rape itself.

This epidemic of false rape accusations is not a chance or causeless phenomenon. The current epidemic of false rape accusations is a product of deliberately cultivated "rape hysteria." The rape hysteria has become a profit enterprise for exploiters in politics, the mainstream media, and in various industries which profit from the fear and ignorance behind it.

It is imperative that we begin asserting substantial criminal sanctions against women who falsely accuse men of rape. This is necessary in any effort of the criminal justice system, to restore integrity to the prosecution of sex crimes, and restore the public's confidence in the concerns of actual victims of rape.

It is also imperative that we begin offering men ways to avoid the scourge of false accusations, and, the equal protection of the laws, by prosecuting women who make false accusations of rape.

Government Sponsored False Accusations:

The second heaviest influence on the rapidly expanding epidemic of false rape accusations, is the government policy of paying money to women to make false accusations of rape.

It may be difficult for most Americans (or citizens of other countries around the world) to believe that governments actually pay women to make false accusations, however, the evidence is not disputable.

In first encountering this assertion, most people reading it will respond with disbelief and fierce denial. The concept itself so contradicts the notions of justice that the average person recoils at the thought that their worshipped government would, or could, be so malignant as to advance false accusations of rape with money taken from taxpayers.

One case study of the government using public money, to encourage false rape accusations, lies in the story of professional football player, Brian Banks.

Mr. Banks, in high school, was a top college football prospect. He played as a middle linebacker at Long Beach Poly High School in Los Angeles. During summer school, he got up from class to make a phone call. While in the hallway, Mr. Banks ran into a high school sophomore by the name of Wanetta Gibson. Gibson flirted with Mr. Banks and the two went to an excluded spot where they engaged in consensual sex. This was in February of 2002.

Shortly after Mr. Banks graduated from high school, Gibson accused him of rape. The California "Innocence Project" describes what happened to Mr. Banks' dreams of being a professional football player.

A high-school acquaintance – Wanetta Gibson – shattered that dream one fateful day after she accused Banks of rape and kidnapping following a consensual sexual encounter on the school campus. It was Banks' word against hers and she was not likely to change her story. After all, Gibson sued the Long Beach Unified School District claiming the school's lax security provided an unsafe environment that led to the fraudulent rape. She would eventually receive a settlement of 1.5 million dollars.

Banks was faced with an impossible decision at the time – either fight the charges and risk spending 41 years-to-life in prison, or take a plea deal and spend a little over 5 years of actual prison confinement. Although it would mean destroying his chance to go to college and play football, a lengthy probationary period, and a lifetime of registration as a sex offender, Banks chose the lesser of two evils when he pleaded no contest to the charges.

Nearly a decade after his conviction, Gibson recanted her statements and has acknowledged she fabricated the whole story. The California Innocence Project presented this evidence of Banks' innocence to the Los Angeles District Attorney's Office who launched an investiga-

tion into the case. After a thorough review of the evidence, the District Attorney's Office conceded that Banks was wrongfully convicted.

On Thursday, May 24, 2012, Judge Mark C. Kim of the Los Angeles Superior Court reversed Banks' conviction and ended his nightmare of wrongful conviction.[6]

Wanetta Gibson was, literally, paid $1.5 Million dollars, by a government entity, to falsely accuse Mr. Banks of rape.

As part of the denial process, many readers will be tempted to declare that the government did not "intend" to pay her to make a false accusation of rape. False rape apologists will "explain" that the government's intent in making such payments is to "compensate" a victim for injuries sustained as a victim of crime. This argument, however, is merely pedantic and semantic. However one labels a payment to a false accuser, whether it is "victim compensation," or a "bounty" for making false accusations, the result is the same – Gibson was handsomely rewarded, by government entities

---

[6] http://californiainnocenceproject.org/read-their-stories/brian-banks/?gclid=Cj0KEQiA6ounBRCq0LKBjKGgysEBEiQAZmpvA20gfuOnQaHMpQTdMV11YMCY7is4lYNBotB2ftH4NE0aAufq8P8HAQ

(through the government entity of a court system) for falsely accusing an innocent young athlete of rape. That the government was reckless in its funding of the false rape accusations is little different than if it had intended the result of paying Gibson $1.5 M to make a false accusation of rape.

Gibson finally confessed to Mr. Banks, and his private investigator, while being secretly taped, that there had been no rape and that the intercourse between them on that fateful day had been fully consensual. She stated, however, that she was not willing to exonerate Mr. Banks because if she was truthful with the authorities, she may have to give back the $1.5 million dollars the government had provided to her for her false accusation of rape.

Heavy government funding for women to make false accusations of rape is not limited to the U.S. Government. The country of India, for example, is required to pay false rape accusers the moment they make a false accusation of rape. The amount of the payment is up to the equivalent of approximately $212,685.00.[7]

---

[7] In terms of real exchange rates, the actual upper limit a rape accuser may receive for making a false rape claim is about $112.685.22 USD. Although a modest sum in the U.S., it is a royal fortune for anyone residing in India. It is at least comparable to the

The moment an accuser files a claim for compensation as a "rape victim," whether there is any proof of rape or not, the victim is entitled to receive 20,000 rupees from the Indian government, payable within two weeks of the false accusation of rape being made. More money is paid to the accuser (whether the accusation is true or false) as the case progresses. The accuser is literally paid to testify against the man she has accused, and, receives even more money if the man falsely accused is convicted on the basis of her false testimony.[8]

The result of this government sponsorship, of false rape accusations, is that the rate of false rape accusations in India have climbed to as much as 93% in some districts. In addition, the acquittal rate in cases that eventually go to trial (while the falsely accused are in prison) have reached as high as 73% in major metropolitan districts such as New Delhi.[9] Of the remaining

---

1.5 Million USD payment that Wanetta Gibson received for her false accusations against Mr. Banks.

[8] Editorial, "*Rising Menace of False Rape Cases in India Problems and Solutions*," 35 J. INDIAN ACAD. FORENSIC MED. 3, Juu-September 2013.

[9] *Id.* Even the Delhi Commission for Women (DCW), an anti-male feminist group in India, admits that 53% of cases filed in New Delhi were false cases. http://www.dnaindia.com/india/report-53-rape-cases-filed-between-april-2013-and-july-2013-false-delhi-commission-of-women-2023334

47% of cases which proceeded to trial, 78% of those cases turned out to be false cases as well, resulting in acquittals.[10]

As a result of the government funding of false accusations of rape, rape hysteria has taken hold in India, as it has on college campuses in the U.S., and in the worldwide mainstream media.

The argument of false rape apologists is that the government's intent, in providing victim compensation, is not to foster false accusations of rape, but, to compensate victims for harm. This argument is specious (*i.e.* it sounds good but it falls apart under examination). When any person or entity proceeds with reckless[11] disregard for the truth, or, the consequences of their actions, then, they are presumed to be acting with intent to cause the consequences that re-

[10] MAHENDER SINGH MANRAL, "False rape' cases soar in Delhi as number of acquittals hits 78 per cent," Daily Mail India, June 12, 2014. http://www.dailymail.co.uk/indiahome/indianews/article-2656609/False-rape-cases-soar-Capital-number-acquittals-hits-78-cent.html

[11] Reckless means: "Conduct whereby the actor does not desire harmful consequence but...foresees the possibility and consciously takes the risk," or alternatively as "a state of mind in which a person does not care about the consequences of his or her actions." Black's Law dictionary 1053 (Bryan A. Garner ed., 8th ed. abr. 2005).

sult. We can infer, especially from the high rates of false accusations of rape, that governments intend to support and cause increases in false accusations of rape, by continuously paying women to falsely accuse men.

Misandry & Androphobia Drive False Accusations of Rape:

In their book "Legalizing Misandry," Paul Nathanson and Katherine Young explain how hatred of men has become an unconscious premise in much of our culture and institutions:

> *Some people are aware of misandry but fervently believe that hatred toward men should be regarded as a legitimate exception to the general rule against hatred toward other groups. Most people find it hard even to notice misandry. The very idea seems counterintuitive. Men, according to conventional wisdom, have all of the power. Therefore, presumably, they are immune to all serious harm. . . .*
>
> *By now, our legal systems are based firmly on double standards. No matter*

> *how liberal, no matter how complacent, men who end up in court over conflicts with women soon discover these double standards not only in connection with custody and child support but also in connection with accusations of domestic violence and even in the reversal of such basic legal principles as the presumption that they are innocent unless proven guilty. Discrimination against men is now so pervasively institutionalized that it is best described as systemic and characteristic of the legal system as a whole. Here, then, is the connection between the attitudes generated by misandry in popular culture and their institutionalization in policy and law.*[12]

Modern feminists, in a manner identical to their "sisters" in the 19th and 20th Century Ku Klux Klan, are intensely covetous of women having a right to falsely accuse a man . . . any man . . . of rape.

The serious crime of rape, as feminists remind us, is not just about sex. It is about power.

Similarly, falsely accusing a man of rape is

---

[12] Nathanson, Paul & Young, Katherine, "*Legalizing Misandry: From Public Shame to Systemic Discrimination against Men*," (Kindle addition) Montreal, 2006.

not about sex . . . it is about power. It is about the power to accuse. It is about the power to raise the hatred and contempt of an entire society against one single man. It is about the power to hold public trials in the world-wide media. It is about the power to ruin a man's life, or take his life, in the shade of the hanging tree, without due process.

Figure 3 –The American Ku Klux Klan, and, the 5,000,000 Women of the Klan, succeeded in eroding due process in the United States by vehemently denying men the right to a presumption of innocence in cases of rape and sexual assault.

A woman accusing a man of rape is the closest thing possible to a witch's curse, in which the mere utterance of words can bring complete ruin, torture and death upon any man the accuser wishes to destroy. A woman falsely accusing a man of rape is the feminist equivalent of rape itself.

For this reason, modern feminists closely guard their ability to falsely accuse men of rape.

Bowing to interests set on destroying due process, and the fundamentals of a free society, our gynocentric governments, legislators and police forces insist on giving women effective immunity for making false accusations of rape. The "reasoning" is that if the government punished women who made false accusations, it might deter women who are actually raped from coming forward.

This type of "reasoning" is like saying that we should not punish people who commit murder because it might result in the conviction of people who do not commit murder.

False accusations of rape have, in history, lead to lynchings, torture and tragedy. They continue to result in brutality and false prison sentences for innocent men, while women false accusers are treated with "chivalry" and extended immunity for their crimes.

Most professionals working in law enforcement combatting sex crimes realize that, notwithstanding widespread rape hysteria, and denial of the real rate of false accusations, false accusations of rape are more common than rape itself. One prominent prosecutor relates his extensive experience as follows:

> *For 16 years, I was a kickass prosecutor who made most of my reputation vigorously prosecuting rapists. I am unaware of any Colorado prosecutor who put as many rapists away for as much prison time as I did during my prosecutorial career. Several dozen rapists are serving thousands of years as a result of my efforts.*
>
> *However, during my time as a prosecutor who made case filing decisions, I was amazed to see all the false rape allegations that were made to the Denver Police Department. It was remarkable and surprising to me. You would have to see it to believe it.*
>
> ***Any honest veteran sex assault investigator** will tell you that rape is one of the most falsely reported crimes that there is. A command officer in the Denver Police sex assaults unit recently told me he placed the false rape numbers at approximately 45 percent. Objective studies have confirmed this. See Purdue Professor*

Kanin's nine-year study published in 1994 concluding that over 40 percent of rape allegations were demonstrably false.

The above statements are heresy to say publicly for many politically correct prosecutors. That is especially true if they want to maintain good relations with the victim advocacy community.[13]

Figure 4 - A False accusation of rape is like the crime of rape itself, except the results are often death.

[13] "Craig's Court: I Call Them As I See Them," ABC News, Denver. http://www.newswithviews.com/Sacks/glenn12.htm

The crimes of false accusations of rape are a direct result of the corrupt Klan values that were adopted by the legal and judicial system, and the mainstream media, in the U.S. It is the Ku Klux Klan's avowed purpose, during the Jim Crow era in the United States, to make it possible for any woman to accuse a man of rape, and, have the man instantly found guilty for summary execution.[14]

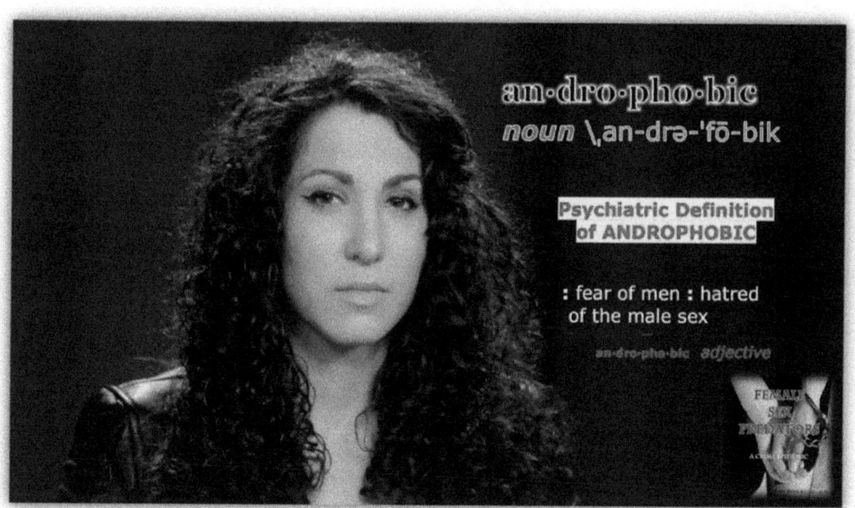

[14] This is fully discussed in a companion volume in the Female Sex Predators series: "Women of the Klan: Foundations of Modern Feminism," http://www.amazon.com/Women-Klan-Foundations-Modern-Feminism-ebook/dp/B00OYA0TY4/ref=sr_1_1?s=digital-text&ie=UTF8&qid=1425399710&sr=1-1&keywords=women+of+the+klan%3A+foundations+of+modern+feminism

Figure 5 - Androphobia has become so pervasive in our culture that it is unnoticeable.

It is in these dangerous contexts, that any man is at risk for false accusations of rape in modern culture.

Personal Risk Assessment:
Am I a Likely Victim?

The first step in avoiding false accusations of rape is for a man to make a personal self-assessment of his level of risk for false accusations.

There is almost no research on this subject available. The reason there is almost no research on this subject is that there is a concerted denial, in the mainstream media, and among most governmental and non-governmental entities, that false accusations of rape are a problem.

The first important assessment to make is the realization that NO man is completely safe from false accusations of rape. Women lie (frequently) about rape for many reasons. A false accusation of rape is the ultimate peremptory weapon a woman can use, against a man, for many different reasons that serve the woman's self-interests. Since the adverse consequences for women making false accusations of rape are low, the probability that a woman will falsely accuse a man is relatively high.

For example, In February of 2014, two men who had been drinking and using drugs, invited a homeless man to come back to their apartment for a meal. There was a woman in the apartment who was the sister of one of the men who had been drinking and using drugs. For no reason, the woman told her brother that the man they had invited back to the apartment was a convicted child rapist (who had raped two boys). The homeless man had no record of any sexual misconduct in his life.

The two men, who had been drinking and using drugs, then proceeded to smash the homeless man's face with a sock containing a large rock, drilled his legs with a power drill, used a spirit level to smash in the homeless man's cheekbone, and inflicted twenty eight serious injuries (in all) on the man. They finalized their assault on the falsely accused homeless man by urinating and defecating on him, then, carried his unconscious form to a closet and locked him in.[15]

---

[15] Mullin, Gemma, "Sadistic thugs beat homeless man to a pulp with drill, golf club and a rock in a sock then defecated on him after woman lied that he was a child rapist, Daily Mail 18 Feb. 2015, Read

This example illustrates a key point in assessing the risk of a man being the victim of false accusations of rape. The key point is that in some circumstances, there is nothing a man can do to avoid a false accusation of rape. The truth is, some particularly evil and malicious women relish accusing men of rape (similar to some of the same kinds of women habitually labeling men as "creepy" or "rapey.")[16] Although there doesn't seem to be any way this poor homeless man could have avoided a false accusation of rape, in general, women who try to label men as "creepy" or "rapey," or, women who believe that rape is common, are much more likely to falsely accuse a man of rape than women who are psychologically healthy in their views of men and society.

[Author's note: Although rape is a serious crime, it is relatively rare in the United States and in other countries. There is a gynocentric movement to persuade the public that rape is epidemic (1 in 4 women will be raped in their lifetime, etc.) however those gynocentric inter-

---

more: http://www.dailymail.co.uk/news/article-2958229/Sadistic-thugs-beat-homeless-man-pulp-drill-golf-club-rock-sock-defecated-woman-lied-child-rapist.html#ixzz3SDWIhEH9

[16] "Rapey" is not a recognize word in any language. However, feminists use the term extensively to express hatred of men.

ests are merely promoting rape hysteria as an excuse for increasing the ability of malicious persons to make false accusations of rape. Our research indicates that it is more common for women to make false accusations of rape than it is for women to be raped. Rape hysteria is most common on college and university campuses, and college men are most at risk for this type of baseless accusation.][17]

Our research indicates that the foregoing example of a false rape accusation is relatively common in the general population. The accusation was a complete lie that was easily proven as false based upon objective criteria. According to FBI Uniform Crime Reports, these types of clear-cut false accusations of rape account for about 8% of all accusations of rape. It was accusations, such as this, that lead to the lynching of over 10,000 men in the U.S. during the "Jim Crow" era.

Let's examine another case of a false accusation of rape, that lead to the murder of the falsely accused, because of "lynch mob mentality" coupled with jealousy.

---

[17] The author explains this phenomenon of "rape hysteria," in-depth, in another book in the female sex predator series: Davis BA, JD, LLM, John, RAPE HYSTERIA: LYING WITH RAPE STATISTICS, Old Town, New York (2014).

According to news sources, a woman aged 31, by the name of Dominique Vasquez, had a "boyfriend" by the name of Abraham Stine (age: 39). Stine had known violent tendencies and had previously been discharged from his employment because of his violent tendencies. Vasquez decided to terminate her relationship with Stine, and, at the same time, start a sexual relationship with Stine's cousin.

At one point in this scenario, Vasquez was having consensual sex with Stine's cousin in a hotel room. Stine saw the two of them having sex while he was peering through a hotel window. Vasquez, through an intermediary, told Stine that it wasn't consensual sex, but, that Stine's cousin had raped her. At this point, Stine, who was a very large man, crashed through the window in the hotel and beat his cousin unconscious. Witnesses said that he continued beating the man, who had been falsely accused, for five or ten minutes after the victim had become motionless. The victim of the false accusation died.[18]

---

[18] Jerzy Shedlock, "*Charges: Murder in Fairbanks result of false rape accusation*," Alaska Dispatch News, January 8, 2015. http://www.adn.com/article/20150108/charges-murder-fairbanks-result-false-rape-accusation

Figure 6 - False accusations of Rape *ARE* sexual violence against men equivalent to the violence of rape itself.

We should not, for one second, assign any blame to the victim in this case. The man was within his legal rights to have consensual sex with a woman. Nonetheless, we can learn from this example about the increased risk the victim had for a false accusation of rape.

First, let's note that the characteristics of the woman who made the false accusation. The most important thing to note is that she was having sex with more than one man at a time. When a woman is having sex with more than one man at a time, that means that the woman can pit the emotions of one man, against the other man, to the detriment of both men. In this case, it was relatively easy for the woman to make a false accusation of rape, against the victim, in order to avoid the consequences of her (violent) "boyfriend" finding out that she was "cheating on him."

The lesson to be learned from this is that if a man chooses to have sex with a woman who has other intimate partners, then that man is inviting all of the problems the woman has with the other partners into his own relationship with the woman. This increases a man's risk of being the victim of false accusations of rape.

Second, according to newspaper accounts of the investigation:

> *An investigation revealed Abraham Stine, 39, of Barrow, assaulted Lord while*

> *Stine's girlfriend, Dominique Vasquez, 31 and also of Barrow, "tried to cover Lord's* [the victim of the false rape accusation] *mouth so his voice could not be heard," according to the dispatch.*[19]

One might wonder how someone could be so evil or malicious as to falsely accuse a man of rape, then, try to silence his screams for help while her boyfriend is beating the man to death because of the false accusation. This behavior on the part of the woman demonstrates a level of treachery rarely found in human history among its most evil figures. It is imperative that a man should never underestimate a woman's capacity for harm to him. The valuable point a man can learn, from this tragic case study, is to know the persons with whom you are intimate.

A woman this malicious, and this treacherous, over a relatively short time is going to give clues as to the depth of her depravity with regard to men. A woman like this is likely to express contempt for men, or, at least for other men in her life, during her casual conversations. A woman like this is likely to be judgmental

---

[19] Jerzy Shedlock, "*Troopers: Barrow couple charged with Fairbanks murder*" Alaska Dispatch News, January 7, 2015. http://www.adn.com/article/20150107/troopers-barrow-couple-charged-fairbanks-murder

about individual men in her life, rating them for their masculine prowess or lack of it. A woman like this does not have any respect for men, and, is likely to indicate her lack of respect for men in her everyday conversations. A woman such as this will find large amounts of fault with men, as a gender – any man she is with might be tempted to think that he is exempt from her judgments. In reality, however, she holds contempt for all men, including those with who she is intimate. Among other characteristics, a woman such as this is likely to brag about her ability to manipulate men, and, her ability to best men in arguments regarding gender issues.

These are all clues one can garner from casual conversations with women, over a relatively short period of time. By listening to how women talk about rape, sex, and men in general, a man can determine if the woman is someone to avoid. If she speaks badly about men in general, or the men in her life, then she is a woman who is much more likely to make false accusations of rape than a woman who has a healthy viewpoint on men and heterosexual relationships.

For example, a woman who claims that men are "coming on to her" or that men are "creepy" or that someone tried to "hit on her" is likely to be a woman who is looking for excuses to falsely accuse a man of rape or sexual assault. A woman who claims that she can't walk to the end of the block without being "groped" is probably a woman who is so self-absorbed, and, so narcissistic, that she secretly looks for excuses to accuse men of rape. Women like this fantasize about being able to accuse men of rape because it is flattering to her to be the object of men's sexuality (her protests to the contrary notwithstanding).

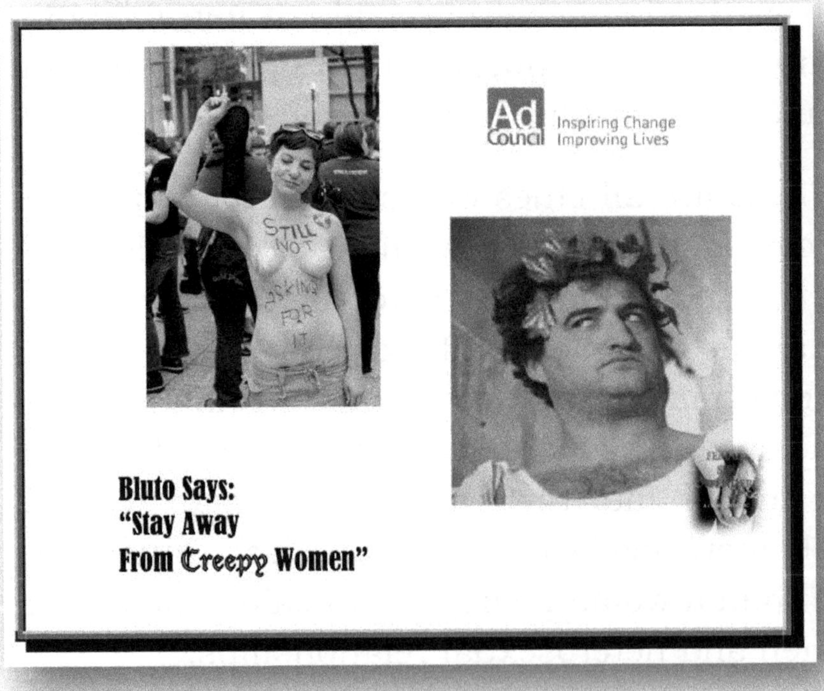

Figure 7 – Facebook meme exposing women who are obsessed with rape and making accusations of rape. The woman in the photo is a professor of philosophy at a prominent

college. It is obvious that men should avoid such a woman as she, literally, is fantasizing about falsely accusing men of rape or sexual assault as a form of ego enhancement (narcissism).

Women who have healthy perspectives on intimacy and interpersonal relationships do not act like the woman in the meme above. Women who conduct themselves as the woman is conducting herself in the above meme, are likely to make false accusations of rape against a man.

We will cover the specific traits of narcissists, and the specific traits of women who are likely to make false accusations of rape in later sections.

College Men are at Extreme Risk [Affirmative Consent]

In recent years, men who are attending colleges and universities have incurred an exponential rise in the risk of being falsely accused of rape.

Colleges and Universities, driven by nothing

more than money extended to them under federal and state programs, have become hostile environments to men in general. Not surprisingly, the number of men graduating from colleges and universities has plummeted. Colleges and Universities in the U.S., because of hostility towards men, now only have as low as one third of their graduates as men.

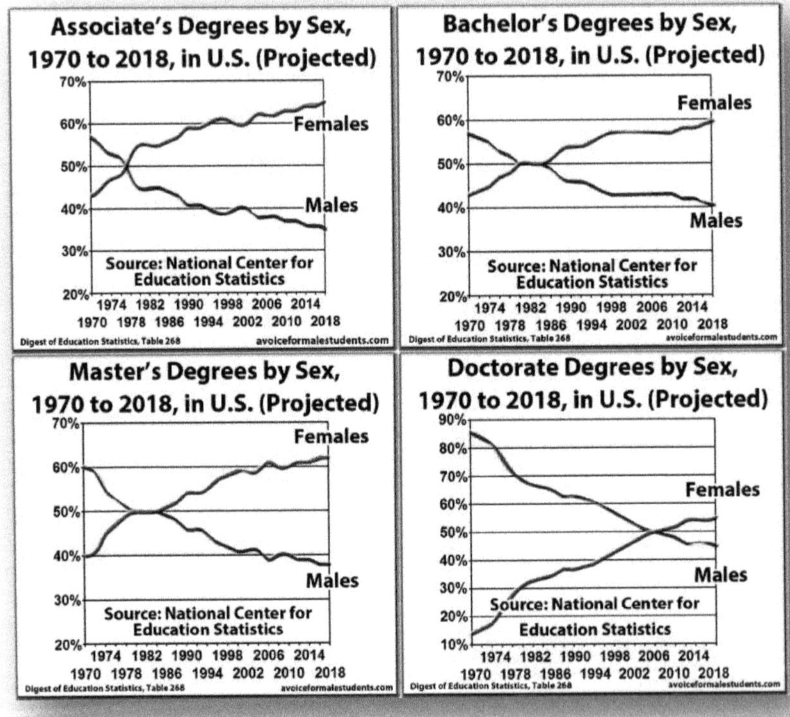

Figure 8 - GRAPHS showing the effects on graduation rates of men v women in colleges as a result of learning environments that are hostile to men.

As part of the higher education industry's competition for federal and state funding, colleges and universities have undertaken a campaign to demonize men, and their sexuality.

Let's take a look at two examples of higher education demonizing men and their sexuality.

The first example occurred at Columbia University. A young foreign exchange student from Germany (it is our policy to protect the name and identity of men who are falsely accused) entered into a consensual relationship with a college woman by the name of Emma Sulkowicz (pronounced: Suk-a-vich).

Sulkowicz claims that on August 27, 2012, she started a consensual sexual episode with the foreign exchange student. Three months after the episode, however, after she discovered that the foreign exchange student had shared sex with two other college women, Sulkowicz then claimed that the sexual encounter in August of 27, 2012 was a terrifyingly violent encounter in which the exchange student choked her, punched her in the stomach, and forced her to have anal sex.

Columbia University conducted a full investigation and determined that there had been no violence with either Sulkowicz or the two other women with whom the exchange student had shared intimacy. The University found that the encounters between the exchange student and the three women had been consensual.

In May of 2014, enraged by the University extending due process to the exchange student, Sulkowicz filed a police complaint against the man. However, the police found no evidence to press any charges against the exchange student for any criminal sexual misconduct. [20] (In fact, the majority of accusations of rape do not have evidence to support charges of rape or sexual assault. Of the cases in which there is sufficient evidence to file criminal charges, or proceed to a trial, one-half of those cases result in acquittals (i.e. the accused is innocent).[21]

---

[20] Young, Catherine, "Columbia Student: I Didn't Rape Her," The Daily Beast, February 3, 2015). http://www.thedailybeast.com/articles/2015/02/03/columbia-student-i-didn-t-rape-her.html

[21] "Complaints of all Crime Index offenses made to law enforcement agencies which are found to be false or baseless can be "unfounded" and excluded from crime counts. A higher percentage of complaints of forcible rape are determined "unfounded," or found by investigation to be false, than for any other Index crime. While the average of "unfounded" rates for all Crime Index offenses was 2 percent in 1997, 8 percent of forcible rape complaints were "unfounded" for the same timeframe."

The national media responded in an uproar of rape hysteria. The media, women's groups, and more than a few government offices decried and demonized Columbia's willingness to give the exchange student the benefit of due process and a fair hearing. Headlines read, across the nation and across the globe, that campuses in the U.S. are hotbeds of "rape culture" and that 1 in 5 women on college campuses will be raped by the time they graduate.

The false accuser, Sulkowicz, began carrying her mattress around the campus, in order to garner attention for herself. To gain extra credit for her performance art class, and, to embarrass Columbia University for giving due process to the accused, Sulkowicz has stated that she will carry around the mattress on campus until Columbia University expels "her rapist."

FBI, Uniform Crime Reports for the United states 1997, p. 26. "Nationally, over half of the forcible rapes reported to law enforcement were cleared by arrest or exceptional means during 1997. At 55 percent for suburban counties and 52 percent for rural counties, county law enforcement clearance rates were slightly higher than the city law enforcement clearance rate at 50 percent. (See Table 25.)" *Id.* In other words, although 8% of rape accusations were definitively determined to be false beyond any doubt, approximately 50% of the remaining accusations of rape had no evidence on which to make an arrest.

Figure 9 - Emma Sulkowicz carries her mattress around Columbia University to protest the University's decision to give a man she falsely accused of rape the benefits of due process. False accusers frequently fit the profile of someone with Histrionic Personality Disorder (HPD) in which the person with the disorder is uncomfortable in situations in which she is not the center of attention.

None of the media hysterics were founded, in any rational sense, on reality.

First, the actual rate of rape on college campuses is lower than it is in the general population.[22]

---

[22] Lydia DePillis, "*Rape on campus: Not as prevalent as it is off campus*," The Washington Post, December 19, 2014.

Second, according to FBI reports, there were, in 2010 for example, only 485 cases of known or reported rapes on U.S. Campuses. The odds of a woman being raped on a U.S. college campus is less than 1:25,000.

1 in 5 women raped on College Campuses?

F.B.I Stats Confirm that in 2010 There were a TOTAL of 485 known rapes on all U. S. College Campuses COMBINED

[Source: FBI Statistics on Offenses Known to Law Enforcement by State by University and College 2010]

End Rape Hysteria

Third, the basis of the media hysteria was falsified statistics promoted by numerous gyno-

---

http://www.washingtonpost.com/news/storyline/wp/2014/12/19/rape-on-campus-not-as-prevalent-as-it-is-off-campus/

centric and feminist bureaus and agencies. The statistic of 1 in 5 women being raped on college campuses included a man making a clumsy attempt to kiss a woman as "rape." Or, it included men complimenting a woman on her appearance as a "mini-rape," rape or sexual assault. Professor Camille Paglia,[23] a mature and well-respected academic commentator on rape hysteria, describes the type of gynocentric hysteria that leads to falsified statistics on rape on college campuses (as well as in other locations in our culture). Dr. Paglia related this anecdote on a PBS broadcast.

> *MS. PAGLIA: Well, one of the things that got me pilloried from coast to coast was when I wrote a piece on date rape for Newsday in January of 1991. It got picked up by the wire services, and the torrent of abuse that poured in. I want women to fend for themselves. That essay that I wrote on rape begins with the line 'Rape is an outrage that cannot be tolerated in civilized society.' I absolutely abhor this broadening of the idea of rape, which is an atrocity, to those things that go wrong on a date --acquaintances, you know, little things, miscommunications -- on pampered elite college campuses.*

---

[23] Professor of Humanities at the University of the Arts in Philadelphia.

> *MS. SOMMERS: I interviewed a young women at the University of Pennsylvania who came in in a short skirt and she was in the Women's Center, and I think she thought I was one of the sisterhood. And she said, 'Oh, I just suffered a mini-rape.' And I said, 'What happened?' And she said, 'A boy walked by me and said, `Nice legs'. 'You know? And that -- and this young woman considers this a form of rape!*
>
> *MS. PAGLIA: That's right.*[24]

Obviously, a college man, attending college, would want to completely avoid intimacy with any woman who believes that a compliment is a form of rape. Such a woman has no intention of respecting a man's sexuality, or his feelings. Such a woman has a borderline personality disorder and is at least borderline narcissistic. Such a woman is going be, literally, fantasizing about opportunities to [falsely] accuse men of rape.

College men must also be aware, to avoid false accusations of rape, that there are entire groups of hundreds (sometimes thousands) of people on college campuses that meet regularly

---

[24] http://www.pbs.org/thinktank/transcript132.html

to find excuses to accuse men of rape, and, encourage women to file false accusations of rape. Some of the groups are in the College or University administration itself. A man in college must now not only be careful of having intimacy with a woman who is likely to make false accusations of rape, a college man must now be aware that someone who knows almost nothing about his intimate encounter with a woman may take it upon themselves to accuse the man, falsely, of raping his intimate partner.[25]

[25] A good example of a false accusation of rape originating from someone in the college administration, as opposed to the woman who shared intimacy with the falsely accused, occurred on the Ohio University campus in the fall of 2013. During a bout of campus celebrations (involving alcohol of course) a young man publicly performed cunnilingus on a young college woman. The young college woman fully consented to the act. Nevertheless, one of the college administrators falsely accused the young man of raping the young woman (see photo of the actual purported “rape” below).

It is wise to avoid intimacy or even socializing with any women, on campus, who have any ties to fanatical college staff, or gynocentric groups which pretend to be sources of expertise on "campus rape," "rape survival," or campus "rape culture." Such groups are effectively out of touch with reality. The mere presence of such groups, or an intimate partner's mere association with such groups, dramatically increases the likelihood that a college man will be falsely accused of rape or sexual misconduct.

The event made national headlines as an example of "rape culture" on college campuses leading to rape of college women . . . . This farce continued in the mainstream media until social media began circulating video of the public cunnilingus, and, it became clear that there was nothing even remotely suggesting that a rape had occurred. http://www.avoiceformalestudents.com/ohio-university-rape-false-scandal-jenny-hall-jones/

Affirmative Consent Laws – [Special Notes on College Men at risk].

There is a great deal of confusion and misapprehension in the media, and among college students, about "affirmative consent laws" or "Yes means Yes" laws.

The most important concept to comprehend about affirmative consent laws is that they are not (yet) criminal laws. They do not (yet) affect the ease with which a man can be falsely charged or convicted of rape under criminal laws.

Nevertheless, affirmative consent laws are likely to become *de rigeur* for college campuses in the U.S. Because of the likelihood that these laws will become commonplace on campuses, we are devoting an entire chapter to affirmative consent laws, below.

"Nice Guys" are at Increased Risk for false accusations of rape

The majority of men who are falsely accused of rape are "nice guys." They are typically not manipulative. They are typically attractive to women. They are typically sensitive and empathic partners in intimate relationships, and, they are typically accomplished and successful. "Nice guys" are the perfect victims for women who falsely accuse men of rape.

What draws false accusers to rape-accuse a "nice guy" is the same human malice that draws vandals to spray paint a beautiful statue or deface a new masonry wall. Women who falsely accuse gain a sense of exhilarating power from falsely accusing men. The women who falsely accuse are drawing attention to themselves, putting themselves upon a pedestal and a stage, and trying to tell the world that they are so desirable that a man would commit rape to have them.

The majority of men who are attractive, accomplished, sociable and decent people have a higher risk of being falsely accused of rape than men who are menial task workers, social or economic outcasts, men who are socially inept, or men who are not otherwise desirable to women.

Women who falsely accuse men of rape are predators. They look for the easiest victims. Men who are "nice guys" are easy victims because they typically judge women as being always benign, nurturing, truthful, etc.

Like any other predator, a woman who falsely accuses will seek to isolate her victim. She will always want to have sex in secluded locations where there will be no witnesses to contradict her claim of rape. Nice guys are likely to underestimate the predator's motive for getting them alone for intimacy.

"Nice guys" will not think to tape record or video record their sexual encounters. This makes "nice guys" ideal victims for false accuser predators. In later sections we will offer some guidelines on video recording sexual encounters, to protect yourself from false accusations of rape, without running afoul of the law.

It is also imperative that "nice guys" save a complete record of their text communications, voice mails, emails and any other communications with their intimate partners. Many men have been spared criminal charges (when falsely accused) by keeping a record of communications with the false accuser.

Feminists perpetually claim that women who have been raped will engage in behavior, after they have been raped, that is inconsistent with trauma from a forcible rape. The truth is, however, there is not one shred of scientific evidence to support this propaganda.

If a woman with whom a man has shared intimacy, sends him affectionate text messages after a sexual encounter, then, later, claims that the sexual encounter was a rape, it is superb evidence that the woman is lying about the sexual encounter having been a rape, and, that she is falsely accusing the man.

Fathers are at High risk for false accusations of rape

Fathers of children represent a special category of enhanced risk men who are possible victims of false accusations of rape.

Many women who want to alienate a father from his children (as the ultimate act of domestic abuse), or, who want to prejudice a divorce judge, use false accusations of rape as a "silver bullet" to enhance their chances in divorce proceedings.

A "silver bullet" is a tactic used by sleazy judges and trial lawyers to insure that a woman receives the lion's share of property, money, child support, and child custody in a divorce proceeding. The "silver bullet" is a false accusation of rape, child molesting or domestic violence leveled against a Father in order to justify depriving the children of their Father's custody or visitation, and for stripping the assets and income from a father in a divorce proceeding.

The "silver bullet" has become all too common in "The Feminist State."

The concept of "The Feminist State" first arose in an excellent law review article by law professor Linda Kelly in the Florida State University Law Review (2003).[26]

Professor Kelly authoritatively, and eloquently, lays out the vulnerability that Fathers have to false accusations of rape, child molesting

[26] Linda Kelly, Disabusing the Definition of Domestic Violence: How Women Batter Men and the Role of the Feminist State, 30 FLA. ST. U. L. REV. 791 (2003).

(and domestic violence in general). She aptly notes that up to 81% of accusations of rape, child molesting or domestic violence in divorce courts, that are made by women, are false.

It is important, therefore, for Fathers of children to be aware of their enhanced risk for false accusations of rape and child molesting, from estranged wives, in divorce situations.

Two researchers (among others) have identified patterns in silver bullet cases in which men are falsely accused. Ross and Blush have identified the following patterns in these cases:

1. The allegations start after separation and legal action commences.
2. There's a history of family dysfunction with high-conflict and other hidden underlying issues.
3. Again, the female accuser is often a histrionic or borderline personality.
4. The female accuser takes an angry, defensive and justifying stance.
5. The accused male parent is generally nurturing, passive and lacks "macho" characteristics. [i.e.: "He's a nice guy."]
6. In alleged sexual molestation cases, the child is typically a female under the age of 8.

7. The allegations surface via the custodial parent who is typically the mother.
8. The mother takes the child to an "expert" who, after being paid, corroborates the abuse and identifies the father as the culprit.
9. The court reacts to the expert information by terminating or limiting visitation.[27]

If a Father becomes a victim of a woman's false accusations in a divorce proceeding, it is imperative that he retain competent legal counsel. If the judge in the proceeding is a woman, it is almost imperative that a falsely accused Father retain a woman attorney. Women attorneys can be very capable, and, there is a growing number of women attorneys who openly support Men's rights.

Athletes are at high risk for false accusations

---

[27] Blush, G. L. & Ross, K. L. (1990). Investigation and case management issues and strategies. *Issues in Child Abuse Accusations* (2) 3.

Blush, G. L. & Ross, K. L. (1987). Sexual allegations in divorce: The SAID syndrome. Conciliation Courts Review, *25*(1).

of rape

"The only thing as vicious as rape is falsely accusing someone of rape," - Jameis Winston [28]

Athletes represent a special group of high risk men who are targets of predatory false accusers.

Women who make false accusations are very likely to target athletes for a number of reasons.

First, athletes are admired and respected. False accusers know that they will receive large amounts of attention if they falsely accuse a prominent athlete. A woman who falsely accuses a prominent athlete (or any successful and high profile man) knows that she is elevating her own status by implying that the successful and prominent athlete desired her so greatly so as to "rape" her. That is a huge incentive for women to falsely accuse high profile men of rape.

Second, athletes present a group of men who are subject to the intense envy of women who

[28] "*Jameis Winston's statement to Florida State hearing,*" USA Today, December 3, 2014. http://www.usatoday.com/story/sports/ncaaf/2014/12/03/jameis-winston-florida-state-code-of-conduct-hearing-statement/19867863/

are insecure with men, and, women who feel inferior to men. The great Nineteenth century genius, Dr. Sigmund Freud, labeled this phenomenon as "penis envy" in women. Women are often hostile and aggressive towards men, through falsely accusing them, simply because they are envious of the notoriety and esteem male athletes (or other successful men) garner in the public eye.

Third, women often fantasize about rape, and, transfer those fantasies on to men who engage them in intimacy. They are most likely to make this transference when the object of their false accusation is a highly desirable man.

It is this last concept, of rape fantasy, that deserves the most elucidation so that men can recognize women who are high risks for false accusations of rape. According to expert research conducted by Dr. Jenni Bivona, on women's rape fantasies, 60% of women fantasize about being raped at least once a month. We will cover this, in depth, in the next chapter.

Jameis Winston, as many football fans are aware, is a high profile college quarterback in Florida. Tall and handsome, a Heisman trophy contender, and a first draft pick, Winston was in a bar one night off-campus.

A modestly attractive blonde woman approached, and, as a pick up line, claimed that she was trying to get away from a guy who was pursuing her for a date. She appealed to Mr. Winston to protect her from the unwanted suitor. (This is a first red flag of a false accuser – a false accuser frequently fantasizes about men pursuing her because of her desirability, and, ask their victims to protect them. This appeals to the average man's ego, and, sense of decency. However, a woman who claims that any man is inferior to her, and that the inferior man is desperate for her attention, is frequently looking for targets to accuse men of rape.)

Many men make the mistake of believing women when they say they are being pursued, or stalked, or bothered by a "creepy" or "rapey" man. Men are conditioned, from an early age, to be protective of women. False accusers understand this and will frequently use the fantasy of another "creepy" or "rapey" man pursuing her as a "pick-up" line for a man they will eventually falsely accuse of rape.

The woman who approached Mr. Winston with the "white knight" pickup line (asking Mr. Winston to protect her from another man), is shown below. Her name is Erica Kinsman.

Figure 10 - False accuser Erica Kinsman. False accusers typically have HPD (Histrionic Personality Disorder); they crave attention – typically act flirtatiously, seductively and inappropriately, and exaggerate their behaviors and emotions.

Having succeeded in capturing Mr. Winston's attention with her "you're so big and strong" pickup line, Kinsman left the bar with Mr. Winston and two of his friends. According to eyewitnesses, she willingly accompanied Mr. Winston back to his dorm room.

After appropriate foreplay, Mr. Winston allowed Kinsman to have sex with him. Because it was a communal dorm room, thankfully, two of Mr. Winston's room-mates accidentally walked in during the consensual sex between Mr. Winston and Kinsman. Both men were able to testify that not only was Kinsman's consenting to the sex, but, that she had initiated it with Mr. Winston.

Shortly after the intimate episode, Kinsman filed a complaint with the Tampa police department claiming that Mr. Winston had raped her. She "swears" that a shot of whiskey she had at the bar had been "tainted." She went to the hospital and had a "rape kit"[29] executed.

---

[29] "Rape kit" is slang for a "SAFE kit" or a Sexual Assault Forensic Evidence kit. It involves a gynecological examination to acquire DNA samples from the accuser, as well as routine tests such as a blood draw. SAFE kits often exonerate falsely accused men. It is a common pattern for false accusers to have sex with one man, then, to cover up the sex to which she consented, she will accuse another man of raping her. Fully 25% of DNA samples in rape cases, that are sent to the FBI for DNA testing, exonerate the accused man by proving that he was not the person who had sex with the false accuser. "Every year since 1989, in about 25 percent of the sexual assault cases referred to the FBI where results could be obtained (primarily by State and local law enforcement), the primary suspect has been excluded by forensic DNA testing. Specifically, FBI officials report that out of roughly 10,000 sexual assault cases since 1989, about 2,000 tests have been inconclusive (usually insufficient high molecular weight DNA to do testing), about 2,000 tests have excluded the primary suspect, and about 6,000 have "matched" or included the primary suspect.1 The fact that these percentages have remained constant for 7 years, and that the National Institute of Justice's informal survey of private laboratories reveals a strikingly similar 26-percent exclusion rate, strongly suggests that post arrest and

Fortunately, the police department conducted a full investigation BEFORE filing charges against Mr. Winston.

The first thing discovered in the police investigation is that Kinsman's blood test revealed that there had been no "date rape" drug in her bloodstream. This ruled our her main contention that she was raped because she had been drugged.

Next, Kinsman had claimed that one of Mr. Winston's roommates had come into the room while they were having sex, and, begged him to stop having sex with her because she was impaired. Fortunately, the police interviewed the roommate. The roommate testified, under oath, that he had done no such thing. He testified that he had entered the room accidentally, and, that it was obvious that Kinsman was a willing participant in the sex and was initiating sex with Mr. Winston.

The police concluded that there was no basis for charging Mr. Winston with either rape or sexual assault. Because of the publicity and the

---

post conviction DNA exonerations are tied to some strong, underlying systemic problems that generate erroneous accusations and convictions." https://www.ncjrs.gov/txtfiles/dnaevid.txt

high profile nature of the case, the Tampa police forwarded the case for a second opinion to the Florida Attorney General's Office. The Florida Attorney General also concluded that there was no basis for charging Mr. Winston with rape.

Figure 11 - A meme that guidess men to "take care of" women who are drunk in such as way as to avoid false accusations of rape.

One has only to peruse headlines and feature stories in mainstream media to conclude that successful athletes are prime targets for women who falsely accuse men of rape.

Shy men are at high risk for false accusations of rape

A man who is shy presents a special risk for false accusations of rape.

Men who are shy are likely to conduct themselves in a manner that attracts false accusations of rape, even though they are doing so without any intention.

Shy men are likely to be clumsy in approaching women. Many women, who hate men, will use the clumsiness as an excuse for accusing the shy man of rape or sexual assault.

Shy men, because of their shyness, also may not frequently call women after a sexual encounter. Experience shows that the end of sexual relationship is one of the most dangerous times for men to be falsely accused of rape. If a man does not call a woman after sex, because he is shy, it may in advertently signal to the woman that she is devalued or "scorned."

There are many other behavioral characteristics of shy men that put them at risk for false accusations of rape.

If a man is shy, it is very helpful if he seeks professional counseling to address his shyness before attempting intimacy. This is especially true in our misandrist culture which strives to find reasons to falsely accuse men of sexual misconduct.

Assessing Intimate Partners:
Is She a Likely False Accuser?

As we will explore in later chapters, the first rule in protecting oneself from false accusations of rape, is to be familiar with the woman with whom you are considering sharing intimacy.

No one can predict, from just looking at a woman, whether she is likely to falsely accuse someone of rape. The vast majority of women would never commit such a loathsome crime. Nevertheless, there are clues that any man can look out for, that are reasonable indicators of women who falsely accuse men of rape.

False accusers are much more likely to have a personality disorder such as histrionic, borderline, passive-aggressive, narcissistic or paranoid personality disorder. Coupled with these disorder characteristics, false accusers tend to have a history of claiming that they have been raped. In some cases, false accusers are victims of rape or child molesting.

Histrionic personality disorder, or, HPD, is characterized by a pattern of attention seeking emotions. Researchers tell us that four times as many women as men are afflicted with HPD. Researchers also tell us the most common motivation for women who make false accusations is their need for attention. Such women make loud and inappropriate appearances, exaggerate their behaviors and emotions, and usually act flirtatiously and in a manipulative manner.

The psychiatric diagnostics manual provides the following specifics on HPD.

DSM-IV-TR – Histrionic Personality Disorder (HPD)

The previous edition of the Diagnostic and Statistical Manual of Mental Disorders, DSM IV-TR, defines histrionic personality disorder (in Cluster B) as:

A pervasive pattern of excessive emotionality and attention-seeking, beginning by early adulthood and present in a variety of contexts, as indicated by five (or more) of the following:

- is uncomfortable in situations in which he or she is not the center of attention
- interaction with others is often characterized by inappropriate sexually seductive or provocative behavior
- displays rapidly shifting and shallow expression of emotions

- consistently uses physical appearance to draw attention to self
- has a style of speech that is excessively impressionistic and lacking in detail
- shows self-dramatization, theatricality, and exaggerated expression of emotion
- is suggestible, i.e., easily influenced by others or circumstances
- considers relationships to be more intimate than they actually are

Emma Sulkowicz, described above, who falsely accused a fellow student of rape, fits five or more of the above characteristics of a person with HPD.

Borderline Personality Disorder (BPD) is another common trait found in false accusers. BPD is most often found in women, with three times as many women having BPD as men. The disorder centers around the woman's fears of abandonment (whether the fears are real or imagined). Women with BPD often engage in sex impulsively and typically have difficulty maintaining stable relationships with men. Their inability to maintain stable relationships with men almost insures that a man, at some point, is going to choose to end a relationship with a woman with BPD. Women with BPD will typically have some sort of substance abuse problems, or problems with reckless behavior, such as reckless driving (Thelma & Louise come to mind). Women with BPD often show signs of unstable emotions with wild mood swings.

Women with BPD will often obsess about men leaving after sex. Accusers with BPD will often tell police that the man they are falsely accusing of rape left (abandoned her) immediately after "raping" her (when later investigation usually shows that the man stayed the entire night and left in the morning).

Women with BPD will often imagine that a man's caress was in fact strangulation of her to force her into having sex. A woman with BPD may exaggerate a man's invitation to come up to his apartment as a command that either she have sex with him or he will kill her.

These exaggerations are not excusable simply because a false accuser has the disorder. False accusers know, on some level, that they are lying. However, repressed anger, hatred of men, and a desire for power often compels them to continue their lying and false accusations, and force the prosecution of a rape case, against an innocent man, based on nothing but their own malicious lies and exaggerations.

Let's take a look at the American Psychiatric Association's description of BPD

DSM IV – TR – Borderline Personality Disorder (BPD)[30]

- A pervasive pattern of instability of interpersonal relationships, self-image, and affects, and marked impulsivity beginning by early adulthood and present in a variety of contexts, as indicated by five (or more) of the following:
- (1) frantic efforts to avoid real or imagined abandonment. Note: Do not include suicidal or self-mutilating behavior covered in Criterion 5.
- (2) a pattern of unstable and intense interpersonal relationships characterized by alternating between extremes of idealization and devaluation
- (3) identity disturbance: markedly and persistently unstable self-image or sense of self
- (4) impulsivity in at least two areas that are potentially self-damaging (e.g., spending, sex, substance abuse, reckless driving, binge eating). Note: Do not include suicidal or self-mutilating behavior covered in Criterion 5.
- (5) recurrent suicidal behavior, gestures, or threats, or self-mutilating behavior

---

[30] Diagnostic criteria for 301.83 Borderline Personality Disorder. These criteria are under revision in DSM V - TR. https://www.psychologytoday.com/blog/here-there-and-everywhere/201112/borderline-personality-disorder-big-changes-in-the-dsm-5

- (6) affective instability due to a marked reactivity of mood (e.g., intense episodic dysphoria,[31] irritability, or anxiety usually lasting a few hours and only rarely more than a few days)
- (7) chronic feelings of emptiness
- (8) inappropriate, intense anger or difficulty controlling anger (e.g., frequent displays of temper, constant anger, recurrent physical fights)
- (9) transient, stress-related paranoid ideation or severe dissociative symptoms

These lists of characteristics of women with BPD are helpful in evaluating a woman as being someone who is likely to make a false accusation of rape.

Fear of abandonment is a crucial focus for evaluating a woman for risk of false accusations. Many false accusations of rape occur after a man and woman agree to end their relationship. Many other false accusations of rape occur after a man decides that he does not want to continue a relationship with a woman.

These criteria are somewhat subjective and ambiguous for lay persons. Let's see if we can

[31] Unpleasant mental and emotional state, especially mood, associated with a variety of mental disorders.

apply them to a scenario in which a man encounters a woman with HPD who is a likely candidate to falsely accuse him of rape.

A young professional man is in a bar sharing some drinks with friends. There are numerous people in the bar, with about an equal number of men and women. The man is moderately attractive. A friend of his introduces him to a group of women about his own age, and mentions that he is a successful stock-broker.

One of the young women in the group, who is dressed in tight jeans and a form fitting top, immediately focuses on the fact that he is successful. She remains focused on him as she observes him. She orders another drink for herself and begins talking loudly in the group about how she was almost raped this past weekend by some creepy guy who wouldn't leave her alone. With this narrative the woman has seized the attention of the group. Some of the women and men in the group express sympathy, and she moves physically closer to the stockbroker.

The man notes that she is attractive and that she is dressed seductively. She notices that he is a nice guy. She has a third drink and begins touching the man's clothing, suggesting that she is interested in intimate contact. This eventually evolved into the woman volunteering to drive the man home, to his apartment, then a sexual encounter between the two, and then the woman accusing the man of rape.

Here is the woman's account of what occurred: (The woman's name is "Pat" and the man's last name is "Rusk.")

> *Pat testified that on the way to Rusk's apartment, they continued the general conversation that they had started in the bar. After a twenty-minute drive, they arrived at Rusk's apartment in the 3100 block of Guilford Avenue. Pat testified that she was totally unfamiliar with the neighborhood. She parked the car at the curb on the opposite side of the street from Rusk's apartment but left the engine running. Rusk asked Pat to come in, but she refused. He invited her again, and she again declined. She told Rusk that she could not go into his apartment even if she wanted to because she was separated from her husband and a detective could be observing her movements. Pat said that Rusk was fully aware that she did not want to accompany him to his room. Notwithstanding her repeated refusals, Pat testified that Rusk reached over and turned off the ignition to her car and took her car keys. He got out of the car, walked over to her side, opened the door and said, "`Now, will you come up?'" Pat explained her subsequent actions:*

"At that point, because I was scared, because he had my car keys. I didn't know what to do. I was someplace I didn't even know where I was. It was in the city. I didn't know whether to run. I really didn't think, at that point, what to do.

"Now, I know that I should have blown the horn. I should have run. There were a million things I could have done. I was scared, at that point, and I didn't do any of them."

Pat testified that at this moment she feared that Rusk would rape her. She said: "[I]t was the way he looked at me, and said `Come on up, come on up;' and when he took the keys, I knew that was wrong."

It was then about 1 a.m. Pat accompanied Rusk across the street into a totally dark house. She followed him up two flights of stairs. She neither saw nor heard anyone in the building. Once they ascended the stairs, Rusk unlocked the door to his one-room apartment, and turned on the light. According to Pat, he told her to sit down. She sat in a chair beside the bed. Rusk sat on the bed. After Rusk talked for a few minutes, he left the room for about one to five minutes. Pat remained seated in the chair. She made no noise and did not attempt to leave. She said that she did not notice a telephone in *the room. When Rusk returned, he turned off the light and sat down on the bed. Pat asked if she could leave; she told him that she wanted to go home and "didn't want to come up." She said, "`Now, [that] I came up, can I go?'" Rusk, who was still in possession of her car keys, said he wanted her to stay.*

Rusk then asked Pat to get on the bed with him. He pulled her by the arms to the bed and began to undress her, removing her blouse and bra. He unzipped her slacks and she took them off after he told her to do so. Pat removed the rest of her clothing, and then removed Rusk's pants because "he asked me to do it." After they were both undressed Rusk started kissing Pat as she was lying on her back. Pat explained what happened next:

"I was still begging him to please let, you know, let me leave. I said, `you can get a lot of other girls down there, for what you want,' and he just kept saying, `no'; and then I was really scared, because I can't describe, you know, what was said. It was more the look in his eyes; and I said, at that point — I didn't know what to say; and I said, `If I do what you want, will you let me go without killing me?' Because I didn't know, at that point, what he was going to do; and I started to cry; and when I did, he put his hands on my throat, and started lightly to choke me; and I said, `If I do what you

want, will you let me go?' And he said, yes, and at that time, I proceeded to do what he wanted me to."

Pat testified that Rusk made her perform oral sex and then vaginal intercourse.

Immediately after the intercourse, Pat asked if she could leave. She testified that Rusk said, "`Yes,'" after which she got up and got dressed and Rusk returned her car keys. She said that Rusk then "walked me to my car, and asked if he could see me again; and I said, `Yes;' and he asked me for my telephone number; and I said, `No, I'll see you down Fells Point sometime,' just so I could leave." Pat testified that she "had no intention of meeting him again." She asked him for directions out of the neighborhood and left.[32]

Here is Mr. Rusk's version of what happened:

Rusk and two of his friends, Michael Trimp and David Carroll, testified on his behalf. According to Trimp, they went in Carroll's car to Buggs' bar to dance, drink and "tr[y] to pick up some ladies." Rusk stayed at the bar, while the others went to get something to eat.

---

[32] *State v. Rusk*, 289 Md. 230, 424 A.2d 720 (Md. 1981).

Trimp and Carroll next saw Rusk walking down the street arm-in-arm with a lady whom Trimp was unable to identify. Trimp asked Rusk if he needed a ride home. Rusk responded that the woman he was with was going to drive him home. Trimp testified that at about 2:00 — 2:30 a.m. he returned to the room he rented with Rusk on Guilford Avenue and found Rusk to be the only person present. Trimp said that as many as twelve people lived in the entire building and that the room he rented with Rusk was referred to as their "pit stop." Both Rusk and Trimp actually resided at places other than the Guilford Avenue room. Trimp testified that there was a telephone in the apartment.

Carroll's testimony corroborated Trimp's. He saw Rusk walking down the street arm-in-arm with a woman. He said "[s]he was kind of like, you know, snuggling up to him like.... She was hanging all over him then." Carroll was fairly certain that Pat was the woman who was with Rusk.

Rusk, the 31-year-old defendant, testified that he was in the Buggs Tavern for about thirty minutes when he noticed Pat standing at the bar. Rusk said: "She looked at me, and she smiled. I walked over and said, hi, and started talking to her." He did not remember either knowing or speaking to Terry. When Pat mentioned that she was about to leave, Rusk asked her if she wanted to go home with him. In response, Pat said that she would like to, but could not because she had her car. Rusk then suggested that they take her car. Pat agreed and they left the bar arm-in-arm.

Rusk testified that during the drive to her apartment, he discussed with Pat their similar marital situations and talked about their children. He said that Pat asked him if he was going to rape her. When he inquired why she was asking, Pat said that she had been raped once before. Rusk expressed his sympathy for her. Pat then asked him if he planned to beat her. He inquired why she was asking and Pat explained that her husband used to beat her. Rusk again expressed his sympathy. He testified that at no time did Pat express a fear that she was being followed by her separated husband.

According to Rusk, when they arrived in front of his apartment Pat parked the car and turned the engine off. They sat for several minutes "petting each other." Ruskdenied switching off the ignition and removing the keys. He said that they walked to the apartment house and proceeded up the stairs to his room. Rusk testified that Pat came willingly to his room and that at no time did he make threatening facial expressions. Once inside his room, Rusk left Pat alone for sev-

eral minutes while he used the bathroom down the hall. Upon his return, he switched the light on but immediately turned it off because Pat, who was seated in the dark in a chair next to the bed, complained it was too bright. Rusk said that he sat on the bed across from Pat and reached out "and started to put my arms around her, and started kissing her; and we fell back into the bed, and she — we were petting, kissing, and she stuck her hand down in my pants and started playing with me; and I undid her blouse, and took off her bra; and then I sat up and I said `Let's take our clothes off;' and she said, `Okay;' and I took my clothes off, and she took her clothes off; and then we proceeded to have intercourse."

Rusk explained that after the intercourse, Pat "got uptight."

"Well, she started to cry. She said that — she said, `You guys are all alike,' she says, `just out for,' you know, `one thing.'

"She started talking about — I don't know, she was crying and all. I tried to calm her down and all; and I said, `What's the matter?' And she said, that she just wanted to leave; and I said, `Well, okay;' and she walked out to the car. I walked out to the car. She got in the car and left."

> *Rusk denied placing his hands on Pat's throat or attempting to strangle her. He also denied using force or threats of force to get Pat to have intercourse with him.*

This scenario was taken directly from a Maryland Supreme court opinion. The jury convicted Mr. Rusk of rape and the Supreme Court affirmed the conviction.

It is difficult to read the woman's testimony and believe she was telling the truth. She displays classic indices of both Borderline Personality Disorder (BPD), and, Histrionic Personality Disorder (HPD). Her mindset, and her story of what occurred, is more likely found in an episode of "Law & Order," or some other fantasy crime program, than in a real life episode of rape. Nevertheless, the jury believed her, instead of Mr. Rusk.

Let's assume, however, for illustration purposes, that Mr. Rusk was the one telling the truth instead of the accuser. If what Mr. Rusk told us about what happened is true, then, he had numerous red flags that could have warned him to stay away from this woman. Heeding the warnings, Mr. Rusk might not have allowed her to isolate him so that she could make a false accusation against him. Before any man allows himself to be isolated, with a woman, he needs to make an assessment as to whether she presents a risk of false accusations.

The first clue Mr. Rusk had that "Pat" is a likely false accuser was her mention, at the pub, that she was avoiding a man because she thought he was "creepy" or "rapey." Healthy, adult women do not despise men because of their feelings. Healthy, adult women confront men and use adult assertiveness to tell the man that they are not interested (if that is the case). Another clue as to this woman having BPD is her use of allegations against some phantom man to seize the attention in a casual conversation. This woman was looking for excuses to accuse of man of being a rapist, or being "rapey" or being "creepy."

Women such as Pat tend to fantasize about being able to gain attention, and support from others, by seeking sympathy because they imagine that some man (or men) are pursuing her. Women like Pat will often use stories that they are being pursued by a rapist, or, that they have been raped, in order gain sympathy from men. For women like Pat, seeking sympathy from men is a form of seduction. "Nice guys" will frequently fall for this pickup technique from women with BPD or HPD. "Nice guys" will extend the gynosympathy that the disordered woman seeks in the relationship. It is for this reason, among others, that "nice guys" have a high risk of being falsely accused of rape.

Another red flag that could have given Mr. Rusk a means of assessing the woman's risk for false accusations is her claim that her husband "used to beat her."

This case occurred in 1981. This period in Western culture marked the beginning of intense misandry (hatred of men) in our culture. During this period, virtually every television outlet, periodical and news syndicate exploited the stereotype of innocent women being beaten by ruthless an insensitive men. The myth persists in some quarters until the present day.

We have learned, however, that a woman who is a victim of abuse has an almost 100% probability of also being an abuser. Modern research has demonstrated that women initiate domestic violence in a majority of domestic abuse situations, and, their initiation of violence against a man is the single most reliable indicator of them being involved in domestic violence. According to Dr. Deborah Capaldi, Ph.D., if a woman claims that she is a victim of a husband "beating her" then there is a high probability that she, herself, is an abuser and has an abusive personality.[33]

For a woman with an abusive personality, false accusations of rape against a man are a convenient and effective means of abusing that man (or men) within her sphere (dance) of violence.

The next red flag Mr. Rusk could have considered about "Pat" is that she claims that she had previously been raped by someone. A woman who claims to have been a victim of rape presents the ultimate red flag.

If the woman is not telling the truth about having been raped, then, it is almost guaranteed that she is going to falsely accuse men of rape. In fact, experience shows that women who falsely accuse men of rape are usually serial false accusers.[34]

---

33 Capaldi, Deborah, Ph.D., "From Ideology to Inclusion 2009: New Directions in Domestic Violence Research and Intervention," http://www.huffingtonpost.com/glenn-sacks/researcher-says-womens-in_b_222746.html

34 *See e.g.*, "Married mother accused of 'making repeated fake rape claims - including one that drove her prom date to move state after he was expelled', The Daily Mail, February 26, 2015.

Let's assume, however, that Pat was telling the truth and that she had been raped previously.

Any dedicated and compassionate professional who has worked with survivors of rape (whether the perpetrator was a woman or a man) understands the serious psychological (and psychosomatic) injuries that are inflicted on a man or a woman who has been raped.

The essence of the trauma of rape is that the victim loses a sense of interpersonal boundaries. Their emotional set often becomes chaotic (over time) and they will, in the words of one capable therapist, "spike on paranoia." A victim of rape (as opposed to someone who is just claiming they were raped so that they can make a false accusation) will usually display acute and intense shyness, fear of intimacy (such as many men exhibit to the dismay of women) and crippling feelings of helplessness in normal sexual relationships.

---

http://www.dailymail.co.uk/news/article-2655830/Married-mother-accused-making-repeated-fake-rape-claims-including-one-drove-prom-date-state-expelled.html ("'Christina had a motive or pattern of accusing young men that she had dated of raping her and assaulting her when no such rape or assault had occurred.

A victim of rape, during normal healthy sex with a loving and caring partner will often display wild mood swings during sex. Frequently, they will have flashbacks, during healthy and normal sex with a partner, to the traumatic rape incident(s) they suffered. Many rape victims will not be able to distinguish between the flashbacks, and, the healthy sex that they are trying to engage with a healthy and compassionate partner.

The care and treatment of rape survivors (who are not making false accusations) is a subject that extends over many volumes of professional literature. Assisting and rehabilitating rape victims, both men and women victims, usually requires years of skilled counseling, psychotherapy, medical monitoring, re-socialization and often the use of sexual surrogates.

No man, or woman, should attempt to have an intimate relationship with a rape survivor unless they are engaging the help of professionals trained to understand and ameliorate the rape victim's psychological (and medical) anomalies.

With this in mind, we can see that there was another huge red flag that Mr. Rusk could have used in evaluating his risk of a false accusation of rape with "Pat." Pat told him, up front, that she had been raped. If a woman claims, to anyone, that she has been raped, whether it is true or false, it is a no win situation for any man who engages in intimacy with her. (This is especially true in our current cultural climate which demonizes men for their sexuality and despises men for their sexuality).

If a woman is telling the truth about having been raped, then no man should consider having sex with her without the assistance of appropriate professional guidance for both the rape victim and the man who loves her.

Let's take a look at "Pat" in the above scenario. Pat came right out and told Mr. Rusk that she had been raped by someone in the past. Mr. Rusk should have politely and compassionately terminated all intimacy, and any path to intimacy, with her at that point. By mistakenly thinking that being a "nice guy" would solve all of her problems, he went forward. It is very likely that she fully consented to intercourse. However, in the narrative above, she broke down after the intercourse, most likely from traumatic flashbacks to the time she was actually raped, and, at that point, a false accusation of rape against Mr. Rusk became inevitable.

Women's Rape Fantasies

Complicating a man's efforts to assess a woman for risk of making false accusations of rape is the fact that the majority of women regularly fantasize about being raped.

Feminists, gynocentric fanatics and the mainstream media vehemently deny that women fantasize about rape. However, modern science again overrules fear and ignorance in feminism and the mainstream media.

Dr. Jenni Bivona, Ph.D., of the University of North Texas has conducted extensive research on the "taboo" subject of women's rape fantasies. Her doctoral dissertation on the subject has drawn wide acclaim from academics and scientists.[35]

What Dr. Bivona has discovered (150 years

[35] Bivona, Jenny M., *Women's erotic rape fantasies.* Doctor of Philosophy (Psychology), August 2008, 209 pp., 9 tables, 4 figures, references, 91 titles.

after Dr. Sigmund Freud made the same discovery), is that women routinely fantasize about being raped. Dr. Bivona's quantitative studies indicate that at least sixty percent of women fantasize about being raped at least once a month.

Although Dr. Freud made this scientific observation in the nineteenth century, Dr. Freud's work has been actively suppressed in the U.S., and most non-German speaking countries, because it does not fit the popular feminist, and misandrist agendas, regarding politically correct ideologies surrounding rape.

Does a woman fantasizing about rape mean that she is mentally ill? Dr. Freud and Dr. Bivona have answered this question dispositively in the negative. Women's rape fantasies appear to be a normal part of human sexuality.

Rape fantasies, and rape instincts, are normal and healthy parts of human sexuality (even if admitting so is not politically correct). There are many sound treatises and self-help guides on human sexuality that confirm the widespread experience among men and women of rape fantasies and rape instincts.[36]

---

[36] *See e.g.*, Newman, Felice, THE WHOLE LESBIAN SEX BOOK: A PASSIONATE GUIDE FOR ALL OF US, Cleis Press 2004; Comfort, Alex,

Nevertheless, rape fantasies are often a cause of false accusations of rape.

Dr. Freud first investigated hysteria in women who had abnormal physical symptoms of a medical nature, such as hysterical yawning, ticks, abrupt movements, etc. What he found was that, in the vast majority of cases, these medical symptoms were traced back to incidences of sexual trauma such as rape or the woman having been molested as a child.[37]

Dr. Freud initially concluded that hysteria in adult women was frequently due to sexual trauma. However, Dr. Freud, being a consummate scientist, continued his research, subjected his hypothesis to rigorous scientific scrutiny, and, after ten years, modified his findings and his hypotheses.

What Dr. Freud found, in investigating the hysteria of women who claim to have been raped, or molested in childhood, was that the incidents of rape and child molestation usually

---

THE JOY OF SEX: THE ULTIMATE REVISED EDITION, Random House 2013.

[37] Freud, Sigmund, "*Three Contributions to the Theory of Sex*," (The Sexual Aberrations), Vienna 1920. *Studien über Hysterie*, 1895, J. Breuer tells of a patient on whom he first practiced the cathartic method: "The sexual factor was surprisingly undeveloped."

had never occurred. The mere fantasies of the women, of having been raped or molested by their fathers (or other male figures) was sufficient for women to believe that they had been molested or raped, when, in fact, the sexual events never occurred.[38]

These startling findings (much denounced by feminists, but, denounced by feminists without any scientific basis) formed the basis for Dr. Freud's innovative theories and discoveries on human sexuality. Dr. Freud's insights form the basis of most psychological and psychiatric dogma to this day. (Further discussion is, unfortunately, beyond the scope of this book).

The point is that some women often choose not to distinguish between their fantasies of rape or sexual assault, and actual incidents (if any) which have occurred in their history.

Let's examine a couple of real life false accusations of rape that demonstrate women's fantasies of rape underlying false accusations.

The first involves a liberal woman at the University of Wyoming who threatened herself with rape to garner attention, and, express her fanta-

---

[38] *Id.*

sies about being raped by a "Republican" man.

The name of this rape hoax perpetrator is Meg Lanker Simons. Simons was an award-winning liberal blogger as a student. She apparently had fantasies about being raped by another "Republican" student. Consequently, she wrote a fantasy rape threat on Facebook reading as follows:

> *I want to hatefuck Meg Lanker Simons so hard. That chick runs her liberal mouth all the time and doesn't care who knows it. I think its so hot and makes me angry. One night with me and she's gonna be a good Republican bitch.*[39]

Simons then reported the rape threat to the University and the police.

(Thankfully) the police did a thorough investigation, and, through Facebook records was able to determine that Simons was the author of the fantasy rape message. She eventually pleaded guilty to the rape fraud, and received a minimal sentence.

---

[39] Eric Owens, "*Wyoming 'hate-f***' hoaxer adds to checkered criminal past, now attends law school,*" The Daily Caller, October 12, 2013. http://dailycaller.com/2013/10/12/wyoming-hate-f-hoaxer-adds-to-checkered-criminal-past-now-attends-law-school/

Figure 12 - Meg Lanker Simons, convicted rape hoax artist, wearing her "take back the night" t-shirt (accompanied by a male "white knight") and speaking out against the dangers women face from rape threats . . . .

In the meantime, however, the University of Wyoming "staunchly" stood behind Simons as a "victim of rape threats . . . ."

There is yet another current event that is illustrative of the proclivity of false rape accusers to create fantasy rape hoaxes.

A well known and popular feminist actress, by the name of Lena Dunham, wrote an autobiography which included intimate details about her "sex life." Unfortunately, some of the details she gave in her book, to increase the sales, were simply a fraud.

A journalist investigator, John Nolte, spent weeks investigating Dunham's claims that a "Republican" named Barry had raped her at Oberlin College when she was 19 years old. Although "Barry" is a real person, Mr. Nolte, in his investigation was able to prove that he could not possibly have raped Dunham.[40]

Figure 13 - Television actress Lena Dunham - She wrote in her autobiography about having been raped by a "Republi-

[40] John Nolte, "*Investigation: Lena Dunham 'Raped by a Republican' Story in Bestseller Collapses Under Scrutiny*," Breitbart News, December 3, 2014.

can" student named "Barry" while she was in college. Investigative journalists, however, discovered that "Barry" never existed.

Nevertheless, Dunham made millions of dollars on her autobiography which included the details of her fantasy rape by Barry. Her false accusations against "Barry" caused him to have numerous problems in his life as a result of the false accusations.

Some commentators have labeled this behavior as "rape envy."[41] That is, a woman makes false accusations of rape because it makes her feel empowered to claim that she has been the focus of a rapist. Whatever one labels it, it is imperative that any man who is even thinking about intimacy with a woman who claims she has been "raped" needs to carefully evaluate how likely it is that she may turn her rape fantasies (rape envy) upon him and falsely accuse him.

---

[41] Deborah C. Tyler, "*Lena Dunham: Rape Envy in the New Magical Slut Psychology*," American Thinker, December 15, 2014. http://www.americanthinker.com/articles/2014/12/lena_dunham_rape_envy_magical_slut.html

Affirmative Consent Laws:
The New McCarthyism

Affirmative consent laws are a current trend in legislation (law-making) across the United States.

The drive is to make new laws regulating sex on campuses, and, it originates in the White House. The current administration has pressured all universities and colleges in the United States to enact new laws which essentially make any act of intercourse on college campuses an act of rape, if the woman chooses to claim that it is a rape (as opposed to consensual sex). The purpose of affirmative consent laws is to remove any defense a college man may have to an accusation of rape.

The pressure from the White House comes in the form of threats of terminating federal funding for any colleges, universities or states that do not enact affirmative consent laws. There are Billions of dollars at stake, and, there is no question that every state will eventually enact affirmative consent laws to insure the steady flow of federal funds to state universities and colleges.

President Obama, and Vice-President Biden, both have daughters, and, both have expressed (at least impliedly) that they have no intention of respecting men's rights to due process in any matter in which their daughters (or other women) could accuse men of sexual misconduct.

Figure 14 - Vice President Biden, though ostensibly advocating for men's safety from men's sexual assault, is currently under intense scrutiny in the media for offensive public displays of lechery with women colleagues.

At the time of publication of this treatise, only one state has officially enacted affirmative consent laws. That state is California. However, it is likely that New York will quickly enact such laws, under the mandate of Governor Cuomo, and it is also likely that all other states will follow.

For purposes of discussion, here is the California Affirmative Consent Law – known as Senate Bill 967 – [SB – 967 Student Safety: sexual assault]. We will provide a simplified explanation of the legalese after the actual Bill text:

> ***THE PEOPLE OF THE STATE OF CALIFORNIA DO ENACT AS FOLLOWS:***
> ***SECTION 1.*** *Section 67386 is added to the Education Code, to read: 67386. (a) In order to receive state funds for student financial assistance, the governing board of each community college district, the Trustees of the California State University, the Regents of the University of California, and the governing boards of independent postsecondary institutions shall adopt a policy concerning sexual assault, domestic violence, dating violence, and stalking, as defined in the federal Higher Education Act of 1965 (20 U.S.C. Sec. 1092(f)) involving a student, both on and off cam-*

pus. The policy shall include all of the following:

(1) An affirmative consent standard in the determination of whether consent was given by both parties to sexual activity. "Affirmative consent" means affirmative, conscious, and voluntary agreement to engage in sexual activity. It is the responsibility of each person involved in the sexual activity to ensure that he or she has the affirmative consent of the other or others to engage in the sexual activity. Lack of protest or resistance does not mean consent, nor does silence mean consent. Affirmative consent must be ongoing throughout a sexual activity and can be revoked at any time. The existence of a dating relationship between the persons involved, or the fact of past sexual relations between them, should never by itself be assumed to be an indicator of consent.

(2) A policy that, in the evaluation of complaints in any disciplinary process, it shall not be a valid excuse to alleged lack of affirmative consent that the accused believed that the complainant consented to the sexual activity under either of the following circumstances:

(A) The accused's belief in affirmative consent arose from the intoxication or recklessness of the accused.

(B) The accused did not take reasonable steps, in the circumstances known to the accused at the time, to ascertain

whether the complainant affirmatively consented.

(3) A policy that the standard used in determining whether the elements of the complaint against the accused have been demonstrated is the preponderance of the evidence.

(4) A policy that, in the evaluation of complaints in the disciplinary process, it shall not be a valid excuse that the accused believed that the complainant affirmatively consented to the sexual activity if the accused knew or reasonably should have known that the complainant was unable to consent to the sexual activity under any of the following circumstances:

(A) The complainant was asleep or unconscious.

(B) The complainant was incapacitated due to the influence of drugs, alcohol, or medication, so that the complainant could not understand the fact, nature, or extent of the sexual activity.

(C) The complainant was unable to communicate due to a mental or physical condition.

(b) In order to receive state funds for student financial assistance, the governing board of each community college district, the Trustees of the California State University, the Regents of the University of California, and the governing boards of independent postsecondary institutions

shall adopt detailed and victim-centered policies and protocols regarding sexual assault, domestic violence, dating violence, and stalking involving a student that comport with best practices and current professional standards. At a minimum, the policies and protocols shall cover all of the following:

(1) A policy statement on how the institution will provide appropriate protections for the privacy of individuals involved, including confidentiality.

(2) Initial response by the institution's personnel to a report of an incident, including requirements specific to assisting the victim, providing information in writing about the importance of preserving evidence, and the identification and location of witnesses.

(3) Response to stranger and non-stranger sexual assault.

(4) The preliminary victim interview, including the development of a victim interview protocol, and a comprehensive followup victim interview, as appropriate.

(5) Contacting and interviewing the accused.

(6) Seeking the identification and location of witnesses.

(7) Providing written notification to the victim about the availability of, and contact information for, on- and off-campus resources and services, and coordination with law enforcement, as appropriate.

(8) Participation of victim advocates and other supporting people.

(9) Investigating allegations that alcohol or drugs were involved in the incident.

(10) Providing that an individual who participates as a complainant or witness in an investigation of sexual assault, domestic violence, dating violence, or stalking will not be subject to disciplinary sanctions for a violation of the institution's student conduct policy at or near the time of the incident, unless the institution determines that the violation was egregious, including, but not limited to, an action that places the health or safety of any other person at risk or involves plagiarism, cheating, or academic dishonesty.

(11) The role of the institutional staff supervision.

(12) A comprehensive, trauma-informed training program for campus officials involved in investigating and adjudicating sexual assault, domestic violence, dating violence, and stalking cases.

(13) Procedures for confidential reporting by victims and third parties.

(c) In order to receive state funds for student financial assistance, the governing board of each community college district, the Trustees of the California State University, the Regents of the University of California, and the governing boards of independent postsecondary institutions shall, to the extent feasible, enter into memoranda of understanding, agreements, or collaborative partnerships with existing on-campus and community-based organizations, including rape crisis centers, to refer students for assistance or make services available to students, including counseling, health, mental health, victim advocacy, and legal assistance, and including resources for the accused.

(d) In order to receive state funds for student financial assistance, the governing board of each community college district, the Trustees of the California State University, the Regents of the University of California, and the governing boards of independent postsecondary institutions shall implement comprehensive prevention and outreach programs addressing sexual violence, domestic violence, dating violence, and stalking. A comprehensive prevention program shall include a range of prevention strategies, including, but not limited to, empowerment programming for victim prevention, awareness raising

campaigns, primary prevention, bystander intervention, and risk reduction. Outreach programs shall be provided to make students aware of the institution's policy on sexual assault, domestic violence, dating violence, and stalking. At a minimum, an outreach program shall include a process for contacting and informing the student body, campus organizations, athletic programs, and student groups about the institution's overall sexual assault policy, the practical implications of an affirmative consent standard, and the rights and responsibilities of students under the policy.

(e) Outreach programming shall be included as part of every incoming student's orientation. SEC. 2. If the Commission on State Mandates determines that this act contains costs mandated by the state, reimbursement to local agencies and school districts for those costs shall be made pursuant to Part 7 (commencing with Section 17500) of Division 4 of Title 2 of the Government Code.

Let's look at the important parts of this law, mostly subsection (a), and see if we can make some sense out of it.

The first part of the law simply says that if a college or university wants state (or federal) funds then it must pass certain rules regulating sex by college students. The first set of rules is contained in subsection (1) and it reads:

"(1) An affirmative consent standard in the determination of whether consent was given by both parties to sexual activity."

Under hundreds of years of criminal laws, consent has always been required for sex between a man and a woman (although until 1993 it was legal for a woman to rape her husband). If a man and a woman have intercourse, and one or the other does not consent to the sex, then, it is by definition "rape."

What this provision requires is that both parties must tell each other, in some way, that they are consenting to sex, or, it is "rape." For example, if a woman gets on top of a man and places his penis in her vagina and proceeds to have intercourse with him, then, she must first have him express his consent, or, she has raped him. [Note: although this law is supposed to apply equally to men and women, in reality, the gender neutral aspects of this law are a sham. Few colleges or universities will allow this rule to be used to protect men from rape by women. Because of misandry and double-standards, the rule is obviously only going to be used to allow women to more easily accuse men of rape by claiming that she did not tell the man it was o.k. to have sex. The man will then have to prove that she told him it was o.k. to have sex.]

The law continues:

"Affirmative consent" means affirmative, conscious, and voluntary agreement to engage in sexual activity. It is the responsibility of each person involved in the sexual activity to ensure that he or she has the affirmative consent of the other or others to engage in the sexual activity.

What this means is that each person must make sure that the other person has consented before they have sex. However, proving someone consented, during sex, without a vivid video-tape recording of the sex, under these standards, will be almost impossible for most men. To bring a charge of rape against a man, in a college setting, all a woman has to do is tell the college or university that she had sex with the man, and, that she didn't tell him it was o.k. to have sex during the entire time they were having sex.

The law continues . . . .

"Lack of protest or resistance does not mean consent, nor does silence mean consent."

This part of the regulation makes it clear that it is not necessary for a woman to say "no" in order to accuse a man of rape . . . . all she has to do to accuse a man of rape is cooperate with him in having sex, and, remain silent about whether she consents. If she does so, then, the man can be found guilty of "rape" before the university tribunals (which, as we will explore later, are a system of "kangaroo courts" mandated under this affirmative consent law.)

Let's continue . . . .

"Affirmative consent must be ongoing throughout a sexual activity and can be revoked at any time."

What this means is that a man must constantly ask a woman for permission to have intercourse with her, during the intercourse itself, before he is deemed to have had consent to have intercourse with her. ["Affirmative consent must be ongoing throughout a sexual activity . . . ."] If, during intercourse, she is not constantly (without stop) telling him that it is ok for them to have sex, then, the man is committing "rape" under this provision.

The last phrase in this provision is the height

of "*faire le clown.*"[42] The last phrase in this provision (which is also in the State of Hawaii Affirmative Consent provision) empowers the woman to revoke consent "at any time."

To quote Chief Justice Benajmin Cardozo – "There are two things that you never want to see being made, one is sausage; the other is the law."

Empowering a woman to revoke consent "at any time" means, in plain language, that a woman can fully consent to intercourse, yet the morning after, or a week after, or a month after, can revoke that consent for any reason, or no reason at all, and convert consensual intercourse, into rape, on her whim.

This alone should convince any rational, educated person that "Affirmative Consent Laws" are simply about the power to falsely accuse, and, the power to hate and injure men. They have no other legitimate purpose.

This next section of the law makes the following a rule or regulation that colleges and universities must apply:

---

[42] i.e. foolish or clownish behavior on the part of the drafters of the law.

"The existence of a dating relationship between the persons involved, or the fact of past sexual relations between them, should never by itself be assumed to be an indicator of consent."

This section really doesn't change anything about the law of rape or sexual assault. The existence of a dating relationship between persons involved, or the fact of past sexual relations between them, has NEVER ben a **presumption** of consent to intercourse on a given occasion. However, the existence of a prior or ongoing sexual relationship **increases the probability that the parties consented to sex** on a subsequent occasion, and, should therefore always be allowed into evidence on the issue of whether a man or woman consented to the intercourse.

If this is so obvious, one might question why the provision is in the law. The answer to that question is just as obvious. The affirmative consent laws are mandated to be enforced through a system of kangaroo courts, within the university itself, in which the only conclusion to which the tribunal can come is that the man is strictly liable for rape, if the woman, at any time, decides that he is guilty of rape. The persons participating in these tribunals will not be trained trial attorneys, trained or experienced judges, or, people who are well-versed in protecting the rights of both the accuser and the accused. The tribunals will likely be "stacked" with faculty personnel who are pre-determined to be in favor of the victim, only, and oblivious to due process, fairness, or the pursuit of truth and justice. A finding that the man raped the woman is almost guaranteed under this law, and, the kangaroo courts required to enforce it.

Inexperienced, and non-legally trained faculty members, or, worse, student members of these kangaroo tribunals, are not likely to even remotely comprehend the logical and legal distinction between a presumption of consent, and, prior sexual experience between the accuser and the accused. (Because of our poor system of legal education in the U.S., many judges who graduated from law school in the past thirty to forty years do not even understand such a distinction. Such a distinction is in the province of Aristotelian Logic which is no longer taught in law schools, and, which was seriously eroded by the intellectual corruption of the Rehnquist Supreme Court).

The likely result of this "comedy of errors" is that many college tribunals, deciding whether there was, or was not, rape committed by the man, will erroneously exclude any mention of other sexual relations between the accuser and the accused. This will result in massive numbers of lawsuits to challenge this law under state and federal constitutions. In fact, there are already large numbers of lawsuits against colleges and universities for denying the due process rights.[43]

The next provision in the law is designed to insure that a man will never be safe from an accusation of rape, and, will never be able to determine if he a woman's consent for intercourse. The section reads:

> *(2) A policy that, in the evaluation of complaints in any disciplinary process, it shall not be a valid excuse to alleged lack of affirmative consent that the accused believed that the complainant consented to the sexual activity under either of the following circumstances:*
>
> *(A) The accused's belief in affirmative consent arose from the intoxication or recklessness of the accused.*

---

[43] As of February 27, 2015, there were 59 known lawsuits against colleges and universities in the U.S. for violating the due process rights of men accused of sexual misconduct. http://www.avoiceformalestudents.com/list-of-lawsuits-against-colleges-and-universities-alleging-due-process-violations-in-adjudicating-sexual-assault/. Also see, Valerie Richardson, "*Men invoking anti-discrimination Title IX to fight sex assault charges*," The Washington Times, December 1, 2014.

(B) The accused did not take reasonable steps, in the circumstances known to the accused at the time, to ascertain whether the complainant affirmatively consented.

In plain language, what this means, is that a man may not use diminished capacity (because he is intoxicated) to excuse himself for not knowing that the woman does not consent to the intercourse. In addition, the man is not allowed to defend himself on the basis that he genuinely believed she had given him consent; he must still seek consent every few seconds, every few minutes, every fraction of an hour, or some completely ambiguous and indeterminate effort, to determine consent, and the woman must have given him that consent, otherwise he will be deemed to have committed rape.

The next section reads:

(3) A policy that the standard used in determining whether the elements of the complaint against the accused have been demonstrated is the preponderance of the evidence.

What this means is that if the woman claims she did not give consent, and, the man claims that she did give consent, then, theoretically, the university cannot find that the man did not have consent. However, this is an impossible standard for the man to meet in defending himself. It is the man who must prove that he took "reasonable" efforts to obtain the woman's consent, and, he must prove, with more evidence than the woman provides. In other words, the burden of proof on the issue of rape is completely on the accused man, and, he must prove his innocence with the weight of the evidence. This is a "sneaky" way of making any sex that a man has on campus an automatic rape, unless the man can prove he is innocent.

Some people call this "fascism." This completely removes the presumption of innocence that has been the entire basis of American jurisprudence since the Declaration of Independence.[44] This provision, coupled with the other provisions, completely removes any burden from a complaining woman from having to prove anything, other than that she had intercourse with the man, in order for the university to find that

---

[44] In France, prosecutions under the Napoleonic Code, even to this day, do not extend the presumption of innocence to the accused. However, under the French system of criminal law, the state is at least required to produce all evidence that a crime was committed, and enough evidence to convict a man at trial, before the state is permitted to file charges against an accused.

the man raped the woman.

The next provision is almost self-explanatory. It tracks the California criminal statute on rape[45] as far as imposing a finding of rape if the complaining woman was unconscious, impaired by drugs or alcohol so that she could not give consent, or, was mentally or physically handicapped so that she could not give consent or communicate her lack of consent. The provision reads:

> *(4) A policy that, in the evaluation of complaints in the disciplinary process, it shall not be a valid excuse that the accused believed that the complainant affirmatively consented to the sexual activity if the accused knew or reasonably should have known that the complainant was unable to consent to the sexual activity under any of the following circumstances:*
>
> *(A) The complainant was asleep or unconscious.*
>
> *(B) The complainant was incapacitated due to the influence of drugs, alcohol, or medication, so that the complainant could not understand the fact, nature, or extent of the sexual activity.*

45 CAL. PEN. CODE § 261 (2014).

(C) The complainant was unable to communicate due to a mental or physical condition.

What this means is that if the man believed he had consent, but the woman was unconscious, drunk or disabled to the point where she could not communicate consent, then, the man is still automatically guilty of rape if he had intercourse with her.

The remainder of the statute ((b) and the following) essentially mandates that the college or university provide an accuser-oriented system of responding to complaints of sexual assault (including rape). The system the law mandates is similar to what is in effect in most district attorney, or U. S. Attorney offices across the United States.

One provision that is conspicuously missing from the law is a requirement that the university disclose any and all information it obtains to the accused. There should also be an affirmative requirement that the university MUST disclose any information to the student, or his counsel, that tends to show that the accused is innocent of the accusations. The absence of this provision, in the law, more than likely precludes the possibility of “due process” on college campuses.

In summary, the affirmative consent laws, such as this California law, can best be described with the French "*chemin de fer*" – "railroad."

Notwithstanding the fascist nature of these affirmative consent laws, feminists are busy preparing to protest these laws as being too fair to an accused man.

One feminist attorney is preparing to challenge affirmative consent laws because they do not automatically require that a man be convicted (or found guilty of) rape as soon as he is accused of rape by a woman.

> *. . . . Boston-based attorney and law professor Wendy Murphy argues that the problem with the new standard is that it doesn't go far enough to protect women.*[46]

Murphy's "reasoning" is somewhat convoluted and incomprehensible. Much of it is incomprehensible because she is trying to defend blatant misandry, and, because she promotes the

---

[46] Jessica, Bakeman, "*Sexual violence law specialist threatens SUNY over affirmative consent*," Capital New York, February 25, 2015. http://www.capitalnewyork.com/article/albany/2015/02/8562792/sexual-violence-law-specialist-threatens-suny-over-affirmative-consen

myth that only men are perpetrators of sexual violence, and, women are only victims of men's sexual violence. We offer readers some insight into Murphy's "logic" that affirmative consent does not "go far enough to protect women." Murphy writes in a Boston Globe editorial:

> *First, a "preponderance of the evidence" rule is now in place as the burden of proof in campus hearings. Preponderance is appropriate because it is the only standard that presumes the equal credibility of all students. Harvard's previous standard was more onerous and effectively valued the word of a woman as inherently less credible than the word of all other students.*
>
> *Second, Harvard now applies an "unwelcomeness" standard to a determination of whether an incident occurred. This is a vast improvement over past criminal law definitions such as "non-consent." "Unwelcome" protects women's autonomy because it asks only whether the victim subjectively wanted sexual contact. By contrast, under "non-consent" and even the trendy "affirmative consent" or "yes means yes" rule, lack of consent is inadequate to establish that an offense took place because an offender's "mistake" can trump a victim's actual lack of consent. Such "mistake" defenses subjugate women by diminishing their 100 percent authority over their bodies by however*

much weight is accorded their attackers' mistakes.[47]

What Murphy is saying, in simple terms, is that she wants it to be very easy for women to accuse a man of rape, or sexual assault, and wants to convict men of rape, or sexual assault, even if the man was making an honest mistake.

Murphy's views are typical of the blithering pseudo-intellectualism that pre-occupies much of the efforts to address sexual assault in the mainstream media.

Like most narcissists who irrationally hate and fear men (androphobes), Murphy frames the problem of sexual assault solely in terms of a "woman's issue." In fact, current research shows that women sexually assault, and rape men more often than the other way around.[48]

The problem of sexual assault and rape is

---

[47] Wendy Murphy, Opinion, "*Harvard gets it right on sexual assault, Boston Globe*," December 2, 2014.

[48] This is discussed thoroughly, with supporting citations and documentation, in a companion volume in the Female Sex Predators series: "Women Who Rape Men." http://www.amazon.com/Female-Sex-Predators-Crime-Epidemic-ebook/dp/B00OC6LCW8/ref=sr_1_1?s=digital-text&ie=UTF8&qid=1425147324&sr=1-1&keywords=female+sex+predators

hardly just a “woman’s issue.” To solve the problem of false accusations of rape, and rape itself, our culture needs to start focusing on the double-standards that protect women from accountability for making false accusations of rape, and, at the same time, accelerate our awareness of the fact the it is women who are the majority of sex predators in our culture.

AVOIDING FALSE ACCUSATIONS OF RAPE:
Practical Steps for Risk Management

Men who are sexually active, or, men who are in any position to incur the animosity of a woman false accuser, would be wise to follow some rules and protocols to protect themselves from those women who are likely to falsely accuse.

Take the time to know a woman before sharing intimacy with her, and before sharing your feelings with her.

The more time you take to know a woman, and her views on men and intimacy, the less likely you are going to set yourself up as a victim of false accusations of rape or sexual assault.

"Hooking up" is something that most men and women have done in their lifetimes. However, in the current climate of fanaticism and rape hysteria, "hooking up" substantially increases a man's risk of being a victim of false accusations.

Avoid intimacy with any woman who claims she is a rape, sexual assault or domestic violence victim of a man.

Unfortunately, there are women who are victims of rape, sexual assault or domestic violence. The same is also true of men. These victims have had trauma and misfortune and appropriately deserve a reasonable measure of sympathy.

However, someone who defines themselves as a "rape survivor" or as a victim of rape is likely to be untreated for their traumas. They are likely to experience delusions and flashbacks to their rape, during intimacy, and, may transfer those delusions to an innocent man in the present.

If someone claims they are a victim of rape, sexual assault or domestic violence, and, they are lying, then that person should be avoided at all costs.

Avoid sharing intimacy with women who are having problems with other men (or women) in their sex lives.

If you are sharing intimacy with a woman, remember that you are inviting into your life any other man in her life with whom she is having problems.

It is not uncommon for women, who are false accusers, to feel empowered by having one "boyfriend" or intimate partner, attack another intimate partner based upon a false rape accusation.

Rule No. 4

Avoid intimacy with women who do not respect men.

Analysis of cases involving women who have made false accusations of rape show a common thread of hatred and contempt for men, for masculinity and men's feelings.

Avoid intimacy with women who think that all a man wants is sex. Avoid intimacy with women who think that all men are rapists. Avoid intimacy with women who think that there is a "rape culture" in the U.S. or a "rape epidemic" on college campuses.

The vast majority of women do not hate men or fear men or have contempt of them. The vast majority of women recognize that men are human, just as women. They recognize that men make mistakes. They recognize that healthy relationships involve many grey areas in sharing sexuality.

Avoid intimacy with women who have made an effort to find excuses to disrespect men or find fault with men.

Avoid intimacy with women who associate with feminist or misandrist groups.

There are two principal reasons for this rule.

First, if a woman is part of a group that believes "all men are rapists" or that there is a "rape epidemic" or that someone needs to "teach men not to rape" then she is preparing to make false accusations against men – any man – including YOU.

Second, a study of false rape accusation cases shows that even if a woman who has intimacy with a man does not accuse him of rape, then, all too often, someone in her "man-hating" group, after hearing about an intimate encounter, will take it upon themselves to accuse the man of rape by making a false report of rape to the authorities.

Stay away from women who hate men.

If you are unsure about a woman as an intimate partner, abstinence might be the best strategy.

In the pursuit of intimacy, both men and women often choose to overlook the warning signs of someone who is likely to be a problem in an intimate relationship.

YOU owe it to yourself to be careful in choosing your intimate partners.

Temporary abstinence is a normal state for most men. Most men, even the most sexually active at times, remain abstinent at least one-third of their lives.

If there is any time in a man's life when he should consider investing in abstinence, it is when he needs the time to evaluate a woman as being suitable as an intimate partner.

Keep things in perspective.

There are hundreds of millions of good women in the world who hope to share intimacy with good men on the foundation of mutual attraction and respect. Not all women are high risk candidates for making false accusations of rape.

Intimacy is something that is a matter of personal choice. Human sexuality is an important part of our consciousness. Sometimes, in evaluating the risk of an intimate partner, we have to take chances in order to advance a relationship. A man cannot completely eliminate the risk of being falsely accused of rape. However, if he takes reasonable steps to manage that risk, he can still share intimacy with a loving and compassionate woman that is based upon mutual care and respect.

Proactive and Protective Strategies

It is unfortunate, but true, that in our current culture, men must take proactive steps to protect themselves from being falsely accused of rape. Until rape hysteria[49] subsides in our cul-

[49] "Rape hysteria is discussed thoroughly, with supporting citations and documentation, in a companion volume in the Female Sex Predators series: "*Rape Hysteria: Lying with Rape Statistics*,"

ture, there are some proactive steps that every man should consider when engaged in intimacy with a woman.

The first strategy is simple and proven to be effective. A man should fully preserve all of his communications, before and after intimacy, that he has exchanged with a woman. This means preserving any physical evidence, such as letters or notes, photos and gifts, but, especially any electronic evidence of communications.

Electronic communications include emails, text messages, social media postings (especially social media posts by the woman) and voice mails. If lawful, it is a very good idea to record any phone conversations before and after intimacy.

It is imperative that a man preserve the evidence as soon as possible. Many voice carriers erase voice mails and text messages within only sixty to ninety-days after they are made. There are at least a few free or shared apps that can be used to download text messages and voice messages from phones. Once downloaded, these are easily preserved on disc, or on cloud.

---

http://www.amazon.com/Rape-Hysteria-Statistics-Female-Predators-ebook/dp/B00O74NG4W/ref=pd_sim_sbs_b_1?ie=UTF8&refRID=0041QYPPEPHWTDQR143G

DO NOT UNDER ANY CIRCUMSTANCES post private communications with a woman to social media.

Experience has shown that publicizing private communications, videos or photos on social media often precipitates false accusations of rape. If a man chooses to publicize his private life, and the life of his intimate partner on social media he is "asking for" retaliation in the form of false accusations, and, substantially increasing his risk of being a victim of false accusations of rape or sexual assault. In addition, posting photos and videos of private sex is now a felony in some states. The felony is known as "revenge porn" and either a man or a woman who publicizes intimate photos of an intimate partner is inviting criminal charges.

Some persons suggest using a phone, or other device to record, with video and audio, sexual encounters.

Although this may sound like an extreme measure, an informal and discreet video recording of sexual encounters has saved more than one man from false accusations of rape.

There are a number of problems with this strategy. The first problem is whether recording sex with another person, without their knowledge or consent, is legal. The laws regarding this type of activity vary, markedly, from state to state (or country to country). On one hand, a man would not be recording this for any illegal or immoral purposes – he would be recording it solely for self-defense against a false accusation of rape. On the other hand, misandry is of such force in our culture that any laws prohibiting recording sound or video, without the knowledge and consent of another person, are likely to be used against a man if he successfully defends himself by producing a recording of the sexual event.

No one should attempt this strategy without evaluating the legality of recording their sexual encounters. This evaluation can only be performed by a competent, experienced and licensed legal professional in the jurisdiction where the recording occurs.

If for any reason you record your sexual encounter(s) it is vital that the recording never be disclosed to anyone except your defense attorney in the event you are falsely accused. A competent and experienced defense counsel may be able to produce the recording, in a criminal or civil proceeding, solely for the purpose of defending against a false accusation of rape. Disclosed, in a formal proceeding, solely for this purpose, may vitiate any criminal liability that a man might have had for making the recording.[50]

Above all else . . . . If you have an hint that an intimate partner is going to accuse you of rape or sexual assault, find and retain a competent, licensed, experienced criminal defense attorney immediately.

Do not under any circumstances attempt to talk with university officials, investigators, police, or any other person without the assistance and advice of a competent and experienced criminal lawyer.

[50] For example some states or countries may allow a defense of "lesser of two evils" for making and producing the recording to defend against false accusations, even if the making of the recording might be considered unlawful or criminal. However, these defenses would depend on keeping the recording strictly confidential and undisclosed until needed in a court proceeding.

SUMMARY & CONCLUSIONS:

Intimacy is a normal and healthy part of human consciousness and development.

Our modern culture, however, has provided a climate that is hostile to men's sexuality, and, their pursuit of caring and compassionate relationships with women.

Given the extremes to which aspects of our culture are regulating male sexuality, and, sexual encounters between men and women, it is wise to consider the hazards that attend these circumstances.

False accusations of rape are a fact. They occur more often than most people realize. They are ruinous to a man if they occur, and, it is appropriate for men to take reasonable steps to avoid them.

Glossary of Special Terms

Androphobia, Syllabification: an-dro-pho-bi-a (psychiatric) NOUN: A Morbid fear of men, including coming in contact, engaging in activities or becoming intimate with men.[51]

Gynocentric, Syllabification: gy·no·cen·tric ADJECTIVE: Centered on or concerned exclusively with women; taking a female (or specifically a feminist) point of view. Oxford English Dictionary (2014).

Hypoagency, Pronunciation: /ˈhaɪpəʊ//ˈeɪdʒənsi/

[51] file://localhost/<a href="http/::medical dictionary.thefreedictionary.com:androphobia">androphobia<:a>

NOUN: Less than appropriate accountability.

Misandrist, Pronunciation: mi'sandrist NOUN: A person who dislikes, despises, or is strongly prejudiced against men: the counterpart to a misogynist is a misandrist. Oxford English Dictionary (2014).

Misandrist, Pronunciation: mi'sandrist ADJECTIVE: Relating to or characteristic of a misandrist: 'the university is teaching misandrist lies' Oxford English Dictionary (2014).

End Rape *Hysteria*

Prosecute False Accusations

Sexual Assault
Awareness Month

Also Available

ABOUT THE AUTHOR

John Davis (1953 -) was born in Cleveland, Ohio. He was educated at Case Western Reserve University (BA) (one of the top ten universities in the United States), Seattle University School of Law (JD), and, New York University School of Law (LL.M post-doctoral) (one of the top ten law schools in the United States). John is fluent in seven languages (including ancient Latin and Greek). He has travelled the world over, many times, and has represented clients, in his thirty five year career, such as the United States Government and the Federation of Russia.

He has been a prosecutor three times in his 35 year career. He has held positions such as

Assistant Attorney General, United States Speaker, and Deputy District Attorney.

For most of his career in civil law, John was a successful international lawyer, practicing in many nations around the world.

John is now retired and lives in the South of France.

Lightning Source UK Ltd.
Milton Keynes UK
UKHW02f1929210318
319851UK00028B/1927/P